T0360481

ROUTLEDGE LIBRARY EDITIONS: EMPLOYMENT AND UNEMPLOYMENT

Volume 8

INEQUALITY IN THE WORKPLACE

INEQUALITY IN THE WORKPLACE

Underemployment among Mexicans,
African Americans, and Whites

JOSÉ M. SOLTERO

Routledge
Taylor & Francis Group

LONDON AND NEW YORK

First published in 1995 by Garland Publishing, Inc.

This edition first published in 2019
by Routledge
2 Park Square, Milton Park, Abingdon, Oxon OX14 4RN

and by Routledge
52 Vanderbilt Avenue, New York, NY 10017

Routledge is an imprint of the Taylor & Francis Group, an informa business

British Library Cataloguing in Publication Data
A catalogue record for this book is available from the British Library

ISBN: 978-1-138-38855-0 (Set)
ISBN: 978-0-429-02498-6 (Set) (ebk)
ISBN: 978-0-367-02381-2 (Volume 8) (hbk)
ISBN: 978-0-429-39989-3 (Volume 8) (ebk)

Publisher's Note
The publisher has gone to great lengths to ensure the quality of this reprint but points out that some imperfections in the original copies may be apparent.

Disclaimer
The publisher has made every effort to trace copyright holders and would welcome correspondence from those they have been unable to trace.

INEQUALITY IN THE WORKPLACE

UNDEREMPLOYMENT AMONG
MEXICANS, AFRICAN AMERICANS,
AND WHITES

JOSÉ M. SOLTERO

GARLAND PUBLISHING, INC.
NEW YORK & LONDON / 1996

Library of Congress Cataloging-in-Publication Data

Soltero, José
    Inequality in the workplace : underemployment among
Mexicans, African Americans, and Whites / José Soltero.
        p.   cm. — (Children of Poverty)
    Includes bibliographical references and index.
    ISBN 0-8153-2342-5 (alk. paper)
    1. Underemployment—United States. 2. Part-time employ-
ment—United States. 3. Unemployment—United States. 4. Afro
Americans—Employment. 5. Mexican Americans—Employment.
6. Poverty—United States. I. Title. II. Series.
HD5709.2.U6S65 1995
332.6'272073—dc20
                                                            95-25260

Printed on acid-free, 250-year-life paper
Manufactured in the United States of America

To Sonia

Contents

Chapter 6
Conclusions

Acknowledgments

This study started as a sociology dissertation at the University of Arizona, and whatever its weaknesses are, they would have been far greater without the kind help of faculty, friends, and family. As a firm believer of the importance of structural constraints, any merit this study has, is due to the faculty of the University of Arizona Sociology Department.

Michael Sobel and Jim Shockey trained me to do the transition from Mathematics-as-a-science-in-itself to the integration of Statistics within a sociological problem, turning around my perspective of science. Neil Fligstein helped me to realize the importance of the next step: the priority of substance over the instrument. Paula England was fundamental in my understanding of the problem, the theories, and my findings. She helped me to correct mistakes that an inexperienced methodologist falls into when dealing with a real problem. Michael Hechter and Al Bergesen showed me the importance of having a general perspective of my work, as well as to search for the punch line.

Kathleen Schwartzman, my chair and advisor, had enough patience and confidence in me to help me put together all the pieces: to search for a worthwhile question; to develop my project; to reach interesting conclusions, and to write and edit the whole work. Also, her knowledge and interest in third world countries and people helped me make the transition from my Latin American experience to the strange world of the American Academia.

All these people have my greatest admiration. They synthesize talent, training, and hard work. They have been my role models.

I would also like to express my infinite gratitude to Sonia, my parents, and my siblings. They all helped me bear the psychological costs of dealing with another culture and to overcome the multiple limitations of graduate student life. A postdoctoral fellowship at the Center for the Study of Urban Inequality at the University of Chicago, allowed me to finish my study in the present form, and for this, I thank its Director, William J. Wilson. Similarly, I would like to thank Felix Masud-Piloto, Director of the Center for Latino Research at DePaul University, for his support in the editing of the manuscript, as well as for providing a stimulating environment in the area of Latino issues. Maria and Mervin Mendez did an exceptional job at editing the final manuscript and in freeing me from the burden of the final steps.

Inequality in the Workplace

Introduction

During the late 1980s and early 1990s the American economy again became immersed in a recession (Boyes, 1992). Consequently, it became very likely that the quality of employment generated during this period would suffer, and the situation of the labor force could be expected to worsen. Bluestone and Harrison (1988; p. 124) cite a report released by the U.S. Joint Economic Committee in 1986 claiming that the share of net new employment paying low wages had increased significantly after 1979. Bluestone and Harrison's (1988) analysis shows that between 1978 and 1986, an increase in low wage employment share and the drift toward increased polarization of wages are found among most demographic groups, across most regions, and within both manufacturing and service industries.

However, low wages is not the only way labor has been affected. Since 1969, part-time jobs have expanded primarily because more employers view them as a means to cut labor costs, and not because more workers want them. This has produced an economy where part-time employees comprise almost one-fifth of the U.S. work force (Tilly, 1991; p. 10).

Workers suffering from underemployment, either because of low wages or involuntary part-time work, are more likely to be immersed in poverty (Beller and Graham, 1988). And it has been argued that underemployment and poverty are connected to the formation of the underclass and its high crime rate (Wilson, 1980, 1987). Therefore, underemployment is another dimension of labor force stratification. Its study can illuminate ways in which the American working class is segmented, as well as the relation to other social problems like poverty and delinquency. For this reason, several authors have found it increasingly unsatisfactory to look exclusively at the unemployment rate to measure labor force underutilization (Hauser, 1972, 1974, 1977; Sullivan, 1978; Clogg, 1979; Clogg and Sullivan, 1983; Clogg et al.,

1986). Instead they focus on underemployment, viewed as the aggregate of discouraged workers, the unemployed, the involuntary part-time employed, and the full-time low-wage workers. Thus defined, underemployment reflects a more accurate evaluation of labor force participation than unemployment. It also shows a better picture of labor force hardship across gender, race, and ethnic groups (Clogg, 1979; Clogg et al., 1986; De Anda, 1991) than the unemployment rate.

Although measurements of underemployment are well developed in the literature (Hauser, 1972, 1974, 1977; Sullivan, 1978; Clogg, 1979; Clogg and Sullivan, 1983; Clogg et al., 1986), the relatively recent nature of this research vis-a-vis other economic issues, e.g. unemployment and wages, implies that other tasks have been less well attended. Economists, sociologists, and other social scientists have oriented their efforts toward developing theories about wages and unemployment. Thus, very elaborate theories of unemployment and wages are found in the literature (Hamermesh and Rees, 1988; Ehrenberg and Smith, 1991). This is not the case for underemployment.

The present study has three central objectives: theoretical, methodological, and comparative. First, a critical review of the theorization of underemployment in the literature is performed. Given that the theoretical work about underemployment has been motivated by a critical perspective of neoclassical economics, known in sociology as neo-structuralism, a review of the central elements of neoclassical economics and neo-structuralism is undertaken in the first chapter. Such review shows that although neo-structuralism has provided the underemployment research with numerous testable hypotheses, these hypotheses are also compatible with recent developments in neoclassical economics that authors doing research about underemployment have not considered. Then the limitation of neo-structuralism is shown in three ways: one, that the critique of neoclassical economics has not been aware of a great part of the recent theoretical developments among economists; two, that several mechanisms can explain underemployment; and three, that the alternative mechanisms to explain underemployment proposed by neo-structuralism have not been tested adequately.

The main bulk of the critical effort done by neo-structuralists has been directed against human capital theory, which considers that it is individual investments in education, on-the-job training, and migration that determine the fortune of workers in the labor market. How influential this perspective has become is certified by a high Japanese government official, who on February 4, 1992 declared that the reason for the decline of America's economy was the laziness of its labor force, or put in theoretical terms, the low levels of human capital investments that American workers have made. Following this view, the workers are to be blamed not only for their increasing unemployment and underemployment rates, but for the worsening of the whole economy as well.

In contrast, within economics, sociology, and other disciplines, several different perspectives have developed. Although they all recognize the importance of human capital, these authors, critical of neoclassical economics, prioritize macroeconomic or structural determinants as the main factors to explain underemployment, unemployment, wages, and other labor outcomes (Keynes, 1936; Dunlop, 1957; Killingsworth, 1974; Okun, 1962; Hodson, 1983; Schervish, 1983; Galbraith, 1987). This perspective has also influenced public discourse: the United Auto Workers of America, protesting against the free trade agreement between Mexico and the U.S., argued that it would cause higher levels of capital flight out of America, which in turn would increase unemployment (The Los Angeles Times, Feb. 4). Thus, the opinions expressed by the Japanese official and the auto-workers union represent two different views of underemployment, leading each to a different policy.

The former comments illustrate the political importance of both the human capital and the macroeconomic approaches to underemployment. Empirically, the relevance of human capital in determining the likelihood of underemployment is illustrated by the large numbers, relative to other workers, of the very young, low educated, and minority workers, among the ranks of the underemployed (Tilly, 1991; Klein and Rones, 1989). On the other hand, macroeconomic theories of unemployment shed light on important determinants of underemployment. Keynes (1936) turned attention to demand deficiency. The structuralist economists (Killingsworth, 1974; Killingsworth and King, 1977) focused on the mismatch between skills and jobs, especially in certain regions. And the deindustrialization theory of Bluestone and Harrison (1988, 1980) suggests that capital migration is another important reason for the sharp increase in underemployment, especially in the Midwest and the Northeast, where traditional manufacturing plants are closing down and the service sector has grown up in importance relative to manufacture (Kasarda, 1983).

Another important commonality that the study of the different types of underemployment shows is the predominance of service, sales, operators, and other low status occupations among the ranks of the underemployed (Tilly, 1991; De Anda, 1991; Buss and Redburn, 1988; Bluestone and Harrison, 1988; Schervish, 1983). This result is interpreted by the neo-structuralist perspective as the result of the vulnerability and power of workers, which depends on their occupations, firms, industries, and unions. Thus, under this view, workers are not seen as passive victims of structural variables or individual investments, but also as actors with the potential to organize politically (Edwards, 1979; Reich, 1981; Gordon et al., 1982; Hodson, 1983; Fligstein et al., 1983; Kalleberg and Berg, 1987).

The integration of individual and structural determinants of underemployment in a synthetical theory by neo-structuralist authors makes them believe that their theory is superior to human capital theory, since it can explain a higher amount of variation of underemployment. This claim has been questioned by some authors, both within sociology (Smith, 1990) and economics (Cain, 1976; Lang and Dickens, 1988). The core of their criticism is presented in chapter one. Along with this critical view of neo-structuralism, efficiency-wage theories (Akerlof, 1984; Yellen, 1984; Katz, 1986; England, 1992) are analyzed and extended in the same chapter as a potential explanation of underemployment. Efficiency-wage theories assume that the firm productivity is, in part, a function of wages, which offers an explanation of why wages are different across firms and industries (Akerlof, 1982; Thaler, 1989). In this study, the assumption that productivity of firms also depends on the type of job is added. Thus, a new set of efficiency-wage theories results, which could explain why underemployment varies across firms, industries, and occupations. Several arguments are advanced for why firm productivity would depend on wages and jobs. One type of argument stands on the traditional microeconomic assumption of rational maximizing individuals. A second type of argument rests on the assumption of existing group norms and values that determine the level of a "fair" wage and the necessity of a "good" full-time job. It is this second kind of efficiency-wage theories that constitutes an example of the foundation of an economic theory on sociological bases (Akerlof, 1982, 1984; Katz, 1986; Lang and Dickens, 1988; England and Farkas, 1988; England, 1992).

The second objective of this study is developed in chapter two and it is a methodological one. It is concerned with the modeling of underemployment in relation to the test of various hypotheses presented in chapter one. The modeling of underemployment has involved log-linear models (Sullivan, 1978; Clogg, 1979; Clogg and Sullivan, 1983) and binary logistic regression models (De Anda, 1991). However, underemployment has been defined as a hierarchical variable (Clogg, 1979; Clogg and Sullivan, 1986) consisting of four components: discouraged workers, unemployed workers, involuntary part-time workers, and full-time low-wage workers, arranged in a decreasing order of underutilization of labor. Therefore, none of these previous studies has taken the ordinal nature of underemployment into consideration in their models. In this study, several ordinal multinomial logistic models (Maddala, 1983; Agresti, 1990) are used to test hypotheses related to the effects of individual and structural effects on underemployment, namely, age, education, unionization, geographic region, occupation, and industry.

Chapter three discusses the estimation of an ordinal polytomous regression model, under the assumption that the measurement level of underemployment is ordinal. Chapter four presents a critical evaluation of the assumption of ordinality (Clogg and Sullivan, 1983). The conclusion is that the order of the underemployment categories is not justified, according to two critiques: one theoretical and another empirical. Thus, the assumption of ordinality could impose unjustifiable restrictions on underemployment. If this is the case, alternative models are necessary that take into account the nominal (e.g. region, occupation, industry) and the continuous (e.g. age, education) nature of various independent variables, as well as the nominal measurement level of the dependent variable (underemployment). Given that multinomial nominal logit models require the assumption of "independence of irrelevant alternatives" (McFadden, 1974; Judge et. al., 1985), a hypothesis that may not be valid for underemployment categories, a choice between a multinomial nominal logit and a multinomial probit model has to be made. The multinomial probit model admits the assumption of correlated or uncorrelated underemployment categories (Hausman and Wise, 1978; Daganzo, 1979); and in this sense, this model is more general than both the multinomial logit and the log-linear model, the latter one restricted to ordinal or nominal covariates (Agresti, 1990). I will argue that the multinomial logit model satisfies the assumption of "irrelevant alternatives", which will allow me to fit this model to the data. The multinomial logit model allows an interpretation of my results in terms of cumulative logits not possible under the multinomial probit model. This is a practical advantage of the multinomial logit model over its probit rival.

The third objective of this study follows immediately from the former ones. Once underemployment is framed within four different perspectives: human capital theory, neostructuralism, deindustrialization, and efficiency-wage theories, it is possible to discuss these distinct explanations of the different likelihood of underemployment that exists among various population groups. In this study, blacks, Mexicans, and whites are compared in terms of their likelihood of underemployment. Also, the likelihood of underemployment for men and women within and across ethnic and racial groups is investigated. The theoretical part of this objective is included in chapter one and its empirical complement is distributed across the next chapters of the study. The rest of the research proceeds as follows. Chapter two presents the data and the operationalization of the dependent and independent variables. Chapters three, four, and five contain the discussion of the findings. The estimates of the models are presented there and the discussion of the hypotheses is developed. Finally, the conclusions of the study are presented in chapter six.

Chapter 1

The Theories of Underemployment

INTRODUCTION

There are no specific works within neoclassical economics that discuss underemployment in the same way it has been defined here. However, one can extrapolate the ideas that neoclassical economists have advanced about other issues, such as wages and unemployment to reconstruct a possible neoclassical view of this problem. Once this task is done, one can follow the criticisms that other researchers have advanced against neoclassical economics. The attack comes from several sources: keynesianism (Keynes, 1936; Galbraith, 1987), the institutionalist economists (Dunlop, 1957), structuralism (Killingsworth, 1963, 1974), dual labor market theory (Doeringer and Piore, 1971; Piore, 1975) and marxism (Marx, 1964, 1967; Gordon, 1972). A brief review of this economic literature is also presented here. Then I show how these macroeconomic theories have influenced sociologists in the elaboration of the segmentation perspective whose most recent representants are known as neo-structuralists (Fligstein, 1983; Hodson, 1983; Schervish, 1983).

Neo-structuralism has been a recipient of all the former macroeconomic criticisms against neoclassical economics. Neo-structuralist authors have developed a framework that has been used most recently to offer an alternative treatment of underemployment to the ideas coming from the orthodoxy in microeconomics (De Anda, 1991). However, as I show in this chapter, neoclassical developments have been performed recently that have relaxed, and in some instances have departed from the microeconomic orthodoxy. Among these developments, efficiency-wage theories (Akerlof, 1982, 1984; Yellen,

1984; Katz, 1986; England, 1992), implicit-contract theory (Azariadis, 1975; Farkas and England, 1985; England and Farkas, 1986; England, 1992), oligopoly theory (Ehrenberg and Smith, 1991), and the theory of communication and search (Stigler, 1961, 1962) could offer alternative mechanisms to explain underemployment to those offered by neo-structuralists. This shows that the paradigm struggle is far from being resolved and that attention should be placed to the test of mechanisms.

NEOCLASSICAL THEORY AND UNDEREMPLOYMENT

Cain (1976) presents neoclassical economics as consisting of the marginal productivity theory of demand, and a supply theory that includes human capital theory and the theory of labor/leisure choices. The theory of demand is based on profit maximizing behavior of employers; the theory of supply is based on utility maximization of workers. Human capital theory is concerned with determination of workers' skills or occupation, the kind of work supplied. Workers undertake three major kinds of investments: education and training, migration, and search for new jobs. The first improves workers' productivity, which in turn increases their returns. The other two types of investments may also raise workers' income. However, not all kinds of human capital are equally important in order to increase productivity. Becker (1964) distinguishes general from specific human capital of workers. The latter is divided between employer and employee financed on the job training. It is specific human capital that is an incentive for employers to keep workers in the firm as well as for workers to remain in it. Oi (1962), Rees (1973), and Parsons (1972) find that in those firms where the fixed costs due to on the job training are greatest, unemployment is lowest.

The enormous acceptance of human capital theory, which focuses on the supply side, has made some researchers believe that human capital is everything neoclassical economics has to say about labor market outcomes. Granovetter (1981; p. 17) cautions about this common mistake: "It is important, therefore, to remember that to say workers are paid the marginal product of labor is to say much more than that they are paid according to ability and experience." The basic neoclassical model of the labor market is of a continuous auction between atomistic buyers and sellers of labor. "The demand for labor by firms is assumed to be based on workers' marginal productivity and is inversely related to the real wage rate. The supply of labor reflects workers' utility maximizing behavior in a world in which work is assumed to yield disutility, and is a positive function of the real wage. Competitive forces are said to assure that the real wage moves up or down as needed to equate labor demand and supply at the full employment equilibrium level—at least in the long run." (De Freitas, 1990; pp. 95-96). In competitive markets, firms are assumed to be price-takers, since they face a market wage for labor that they cannot affect (Hamermesh and Rees, 1988). Given this fixed wage, therefore, a rational (i.e., profit-maximizing) firm would add workers only until the point where the value of the additional product produced as a result of having hired the last unit of labor equaled the wage of that unit; diminishing returns implies that hiring beyond that point would reduce net revenues (Granovetter, 1981). Thus, any market wage is the same as the marginal product of labor. This conclusion may be deceptive, as Granovetter (1981; p. 17) points out, first, "the amount of product resulting from a given number of labor units results from the nature of the existing technology—in economic language, from the production function. It follows that workers in an industry with backward technology will have lower marginal products for this reason alone; characteristics of the job rather than workers' skill levels determine this." Secondly, the marginal product is also influenced by the product price, given that demand for the product is linked to the demand for labor. "It follows that if consumers change their demand in such a way as to want less of a product at any given price (i.e., if the product demand curve shifts to the left), the marginal product of labor is again reduced, with no relation to workers' skill" (Granovetter, 1981). And finally, the marginal product is affected by the supply of workers. If the supply of workers increases at any given wage, "the marginal product would have declined, again for reasons unrelated to workers' skills." (Granovetter, 1981). What could all this tell us about underemployment?

A worker is less likely to be underemployed if he/she is in a situation where his/her marginal productivity is high relative to other workers within the same firm or other firms. Following the former discussion, this could be due to employment in a firm with advanced technology, or because the demand for the firm's product increases (demand shift), or else, it could be the result of an increase of the supply of workers (supply shift). Given that workers perform different tasks within the same firm, they could be affected differently by demand or supply changes. Similarly, the level of technology being used at different departments within a firm may vary, making some workers more productive than others, independently of the characteristics of workers. If microeconomic analysis usually assumes that the technology being used across the firm is homogeneous in order to simplify the analysis, it does not mean that analysis is restricted to this type of firm. In fact, the firm production function could be defined as the aggregate of the particular production functions of every department of the firm, but one can analyze each department from a marginalist point of view as if it were a separate firm. The inclusion of firm characteristics in the determination of outcomes is widely accepted in neoclassical economics. Lang and Dickens (1988) agree that following the microeconomic model "... instead of expressing wages as a function of worker/job match characteristics, it is possible to express the wage as a function of worker attributes. Similarly, wages can be expressed as a function of firm attributes. Thus, to reiterate, even if one interprets standard wage equations as expressing the wage solely in terms of worker attributes, it does not follow that they have ignored the importance of 'demand'" (p. 75).

It is important to keep in mind the arguments above, since some of the critics of neoclassical economics are going to emphasize the disregard of marginalist economists for the demand side, particularly, the nature and distribution of jobs (Granovetter, 1981; Lang and Dickens, 1988). This critique is heavily directed towards human capital theory, that focuses on the supply side of the labor market. The basic ideas of human capital theory were presented above. However, a more extensive discussion of the determinants of underemployment according to human capital theory is necessary, in order to complete the explanation of underemployment given by this theory and to frame the further polemic. Education, age, gender and ethnicity are important variables in human capital analysis, since they are related to worker productivity which in turn increases wages and decreases the chances of being underemployed. How are education, age, gender, and ethnicity related to this argument?

Education may increase productivity if a person with relevant education may perform a certain task more efficiently than a person without such schooling (Becker, 1964; Mincer, 1962). Education could, on the other hand, serve as an indicator of productivity (Spence, 1974), since it reflects possession of general skills and competence. Thus, it may be more rational for employers to give the best full-time jobs, or to dismiss the workers with low education, if the employer has to choose between workers earning the same wage and performing the same task. Education is also correlated with participation in job relevant adult education (Colbjornsen, 1986). When the worker has gone through firm specific on the job training, part of the labor cost becomes fixed (Oi, 1962). In cases like these, the firm may try to avoid dismissing the worker, or to assign her/him to low-paid or part-time jobs.

Age is considered a proxy for experience. Human capital theory argues that age, highly correlated with seniority, reflects individual productivity related to possession of firm specific or general skills. Since workers with specific on the job training constitute fixed labor costs for the firm, it is efficient for employers to lay off or dismiss workers in reverse order of seniority (Parsons, 1972) and to assign the best jobs to the most experienced workers. However, workers experience declining productivity in their 50s and 60s, as a consequence of natural physiological decline, and of decreasing investment in human capital, since workers expect lower returns with higher age. Thus, the advantage of getting older decreases with age. Taken together, these arguments suggest a curvilinear relationship between age and the probability of underemployment (Colbjornsen, 1986). The older the worker is, the higher the probability of not being underemployed. However, this probability advantage decreases with age.

Gender correlates with on the job training and other fixed labor costs (Colbjornsen, 1986). Employers, viewing a woman's chance of staying with the firm as highly uncertain due to possible job interruptions caused by marriage or childbearing, will be less willing to invest in her firm specific training. Thus, years of tenure on the job will reflect a smaller amount of firm specific training and will produce a strong tendency for women to have a higher underemployment probability than men (Hamermesh and Rees, 1988). This higher underemployment likelihood could be due to discrimination.

Neoclassical economists recognize the possibility of discrimination against minorities or women. The main forms of discrimination considered are taste and statistical discrimination.

Taste discrimination (Becker, 1971) occurs if employers have a decided preference for hiring white males in high paying jobs despite the availability of equally qualified women and minorities. Statistical discrimination (Aigner and Cain, 1977; Spence, 1973) arises when observable personal characteristics that are correlated with productivity are not perfect predictors. If, on average, minorities with high school educations are discovered to be less productive than white males with high school educations owing to differences in schooling quality, or because of shortened career lives, women with a given education level are, on average, less valuable to firms than men of equal education, employers might employ this group information to modify individual data when making hiring decisions. Viewed in this way, the problem of statistical discrimination is a case of the "ecological fallacy".

Discrimination may act as an obstacle to market equilibrium in the short run. But in the long run, neoclassical economists believe that competition among employers will make it disappear (Cain, 1976). Other structural effects on underemployment are ignored by neoclassical economists for several reasons. As Farkas et al. (1988) point out: "Their theory easily accommodates firms and industries that vary according to capital intensity, plant size, unionization, wages, or other characteristics. The theory assumes that employers prefer more productive workers even in low skill jobs, and since workers prefer higher wages, there is a sorting process in which the better workers come to occupy the higher paying jobs. This sorting could proceed until structural effects no longer exist net of human capital." (p. 109). However, the labor market mechanisms that are supposed to erode the structural effects do not act perfectly. There are several obstacles: feedback effects from market discrimination, information and other costs of job search, internal labor markets, and informal networks of job contacts (Farkas et al., 1988; Averitt, 1988; 1968; Granovetter, 1981; Doeringer and Piore, 1971; Stigler, 1962, 1961). Information, unions, oligopoly and monopoly have given neoclassical economists a motive for relaxing the assumptions of the orthodox model.

Stigler's (1961, 1962) general theory of information and search, also known as "search theory", argues that as long as the reservation wage is not equal to the minimum wage offered in the market, the probability of finding a job will be less than one and hence some search underemployment will result. Thus, search underemployment occurs when an individual does not accept the first job that is offered, which seems to be a rational strategy, given that access to information is not perfect. The cost of imperfect information could also be that individuals become underemployed once they find a job, since the wage commensurate with the individual's skills does not match their wage obtained. In this situation, the individual may continue the search while being employed, or decide to quit if this will optimize the search. If a person is looking for a job, unemployment insurance benefits reduce the cost of an individual being underemployed and lead the person to increase his or her reservation wage. This in turn leads to longer durations of underemployment and higher expected post-underemployment wages. Higher unemployment insurance benefits could also increase the probability that temporarily laid off workers await recall instead of accepting lower paying jobs (Ehrenberg and Oaxaca, 1976; Kiefer and Neumann, 1979; Solon, 1985). A particular form of search underemployment is "wait unemployment" (Ehrenberg and Smith, 1988). It shows up when workers could find jobs in the low wage firms, but would still prefer to work at a high wage firm and wait until a job vacancy will exist, given that there is some normal turnover.

Hall (1986, 1970) emphasizes another type of underemployment, called "abnormal frictional unemployment". It happens when positions are available for workers at their present skills. However, these jobs do not encourage stable employment because they are not part of a structure of advancement. This is the case of groups such as black youth and women, with higher than expected rates of unemployment, due to abnormally frequent spells of unemployment instead of chronic unemployment.

UNDEREMPLOYMENT, OLIGOPOLY, AND UNIONS

Some neoclassical economists do not believe that oligopolistic or monopolistic industries earn excess profits since there is always a sufficient threat of market entry by new competitors to keep profits close to a competitive level (Farkas et al., 1988). Hence, there is no reason, under neoclassical theory, to expect diverse effects of industries on underemployment, since the absence of extraordinary profits may deter these firms from giving their workers special treatment vis-a-vis the other firms' workers.

What about the effects of unions on underemployment? Freeman and Medoff (1984) state that unions exert a simple monopoly effect thanks to governmental intervention in what would otherwise be free markets. Because of this, unionized workers receive higher wages and have more job security than nonunionized workers. Since unions enforce seniority rules, within unionized settings, older workers most benefit by unionization. During economic downturns, senior workers are the last ones to be laid off. However, Freeman and Medoff also point out that union monopoly is likely to be important only when unionized firms either completely dominate a market or operate in a noncompetitive market. Otherwise, the unionized firm may go out of business, since it could not compete with non-unionized firms, or its workers would have to accept wages and jobs similar to those prevalent among the other firms.

Unions are also seen as means of collective voice/institutional response that provide an alternative mechanism for bringing about change (Freeman and Medoff, 1984). In this view, unions have some positive effects on productivity, by reducing quit rates, by inducing management to alter methods of production and adopt more efficient policies, and by improving morale and cooperation among workers as well as communication between workers and management, leading to better decision-making. Accordingly, union rules limit the scope for arbitrary actions concerning the promotion, layoff, recall, etc., of individuals. Such benefits brought up by unions decrease the likelihood that unionized workers are underemployed with respect to nonunionist ones.

Union attempts to restrict the substitution of other inputs for union labor typically occur by means of the collective bargaining process. Some unions, notably those in the airline, railroad, and printing industries, have sought and won guarantees of minimum crew sizes (Ehrenberg and Smith, 1988). Such staffing requirements prevent employers from substituting capital for labor. Other unions have won contract provisions that prohibit employers from subcontracting for some or all of the services they provide (Hamermesh and Rees, 1988). Therefore, unionized workers are less likely to be underemployed than nonunionized workers, unless the threat of unionization in large firms prompts employers to guarantee their workers a deal similar to the one the unionized workers got (Freeman and Medoff, 1984; Dickens, 1986).

Does the empirical evidence supports neoclassical arguments on underemployment? A brief review of the empirical literature next shows that human capital variables play an important role in the explanation of underemployment. It also shows that there is some room for controversy with other theories.

THE EMPIRICAL EVIDENCE OF UNDEREMPLOYMENT

Following the definition of underemployment, the empirical findings in previous research are presented separately for each of the components of underemployment: discouraged workers, unemployed workers, involuntary part-time workers, and low-income full-time workers.

The Discouraged Workers

The discouraged workers, or hidden unemployed, are those unemployed individuals who are not actively seeking work, but would like to have a job. In order to find out what kind of workers are more likely to become discouraged, several studies have been done. These studies indicate that among the unemployed, the lowest percentage of discouraged workers correspond to displaced workers who were involved in a plant closing or mass layoff in the preceding years (Buss and Redburn, 1988). The next most numerous group of discouraged workers corresponds to those who have no work experience. The largest group of discouraged workers corresponds to people who lost or quit jobs for reasons other than a plant closing or layoff. This last group constitutes as much as 60 percent of the discouraged workers in some of the surveys (Buss and Redburn, 1988).

Human capital characteristics are consistently correlated with labor force participation. Those having difficulty entering or remaining in the labor force include the very old and the very young, members of racial or ethnic minority groups that have experienced discrimination, women with traditional child care responsibilities, and those lacking education or job skills (Levitan et al., 1981). Discouraged workers are more than two times (38 percent) more likely than the rehired (15 percent) to have dropped out of school before obtaining a high school diploma and somewhat more likely to have dropped out than the unemployed (27 percent). In contrast, rehired workers are three times (41 percent) more likely than the discouraged (13 percent) to have gone to college. Displaced discouraged workers are three times (30 percent) more likely to be a minority group member than are the rehired (10 percent). Nearly two thirds (57 percent) of the discouraged but only one third (34 percent) of the rehired and unemployed are women (Buss and Redburn,

1988). When they were working, displaced discouraged workers on the whole earned somewhat less than either their still unemployed or their subsequently rehired counterparts. Discouraged workers (30 percent) were twice as likely as the unemployed (15 percent) or rehired (14 percent) to be laid off from nondurable goods manufacturing jobs. On top of this, discouraged workers had worked in lower status jobs than the others. Rehired workers were two times more likely to have worked in executive or management jobs than were discouraged workers. In contrast, discouraged workers were much more likely than the rehired to have been unskilled material handlers, and also more likely than other displaced workers to have held part time jobs prior to layoff (Buss and Redburn, 1988).

When displaced discouraged workers are compared with discouraged workers losing jobs for other reasons, the two groups are seen to differ in terms of education, age, and sex. Other job losers who are discouraged are twice (22.3 percent) as likely to have attended college as displaced discouraged workers (12.6). Displaced discouraged workers are more likely (48 percent) to be male than other job losers who are discouraged. Other job losers are much more likely to be 60 years of age or older (20.9 percent) than are the displaced discouraged (8.8 percent). Finally, other job losers (23 percent) were nearly three times more likely to be involved in retail trade job loss than the displaced (8 percent), but displaced discouraged workers were more likely to have lost a job in manufacturing (48 percent) as those not displaced (27 percent) (Buss and Redburn, 1988).

The never worked discouraged workers are more likely to be poorly educated, to be minorities, especially blacks, to never have been married, to be male, and to be younger (20 to 24 years old) than either the displaced discouraged or discouraged workers who lost their jobs for other reasons (Buss and Redburn, 1988). The discouraged with work experience are at a disadvantage relative to the "core" labor force, which is dominated by prime working age, educated or skilled, white males. Thus, the discouraged workers who have never worked are likely to be the least competitive subset, it is this pool of individuals who suffers the highest hardship in the labor market.

The Unemployed

The profile of the unemployed looks very similar to that of the discouraged workers. Unemployment is more pervasive among young workers. Using data from the U.S. Department of Labor, Ehrenberg and Smith (1991) show that the unemployment rate of white male workers between 16 to 17 years old is 16.1 percent in 1988, while the same rate for white male workers between 25 to 54 is 3.8 percent during the same year. The same study shows the relevance of gender, ethnicity and race: white females 25-54 years old have an unemployment rate of 3.9 percent. The same rate for black males and females in the 25-54 age cohort amounts to 8.9 and 9.4 respectively, in the same year of the study. Using 1987 CPS data, De Anda (1991) finds that the unemployment rate of workers with 12 years of schooling is 13.2 percent for mexican males, and 8.2 percent for white males. If the schooling level is of more than 12 years, mexican males have an unemployment rate of 11.7 percent while white males have a 4.5 percent unemployment rate.

Buss and Redburn (1988) use the 1984 CPS and Plant Closing Supplement Data to show that the unemployed due to layoffs are unequally distributed across industrial sectors. Those industrial sectors with the highest unemployment rates are construction (7.8 percent), manufacture-durable (18.4 percent), manufacture-non-durable (29.9 percent), wholesale and retail sales (11.2 percent), and public administration (9.3 percent). These same authors also show that occupations differ in unemployment rates; sales (11.8 percent), clerical (15.7 percent), and operators (21.5 percent) the highest. Executives and managers (1.9 percent), professionals (5.6 percent), and technicians (0.0 percent) have the lowest unemployment rate.

Involuntary Part-Time Workers

Part-time employees comprise almost one fifth of the U.S. work force. Of the 2.6 percentage point increase in the rate of part-time employment between 1969 and 1989, 1.7 percentage points are accounted for by growth in involuntary part-time work. In other words, companies are creating part-time jobs even though workers do not want them (Tilly, 1991). As is true for people on full-time schedules, the majority of persons working part-time involuntarily who usually work full-time are men. In contrast, the majority of those who usually work part-time, voluntarily or involuntarily, are women, two-thirds of the total part-time workers in 1985 (Nardone, 1986). While most women who are employed part-time are married, most men are single (Nardone, 1986).

In 1985, 6.3 million people between the ages of 16 and 24 were in school and employed. About four-fifths of these worked part-time. Among those who worked but were not enrolled in school, fewer than 15 percent were part-timers. Part-time schedules are attractive to older workers, who use them to ease the transition into retirement. These jobs also provide supplementary retirement income (Nardone, 1986).

In 1985, a slightly higher proportion of whites than blacks were employed part-time, 18 against 16 percent, men and women combined. This difference was greater among women than men, 28 versus 20 percent, whites and blacks combined (Nardone, 1986).

Almost two-thirds of all part-timers work in clerical, sales, and service occupations. These occupations are predominantly low-paid and low-skilled compared to managers, professionals, and technicians (Hinojosa-Ojeda et al., 1991). Even full-time clerical workers earn only 83 percent of the median full-time weekly wage; service workers earn 64 percent; and sales workers just come out equal to the median. In addition, part-time workers are much less likely to receive most major fringe benefits than are full-timers. The average job tenure of a part-time worker is 3.4 years, while the average of full-time working women is 5.7 years, and the average of full-time working men is 8.1 years (Tilly, 1991). Part-time workers are more apt than their full-time counterparts to hold jobs in retail trade and service industries. Together, these industries accounted for 79 percent of the part-time nonagricultural wage and salary workers (Nardone, 1986).

Blank (1990) suggests that part-time workers are worse off because they have some negative unmeasured productivity characteristics, which may also be the reason they are unable to find full-time work. Tilly (1991) believes a more likely reason for employers to increase the amount of part-time jobs is due to the costs of fringe benefits, which rose from 28 percent of total compensation in 1969 to 37 percent in 1988. Because part-time workers are much less likely to receive fringe benefits than are full-timers, employers may be hiring more part-timers to minimize benefits costs. However, Tilly's data analysis does not support this hypothesis. It supports the alternative explanation that the industry composition has shifted away from manufacturing and toward industries such as trade and services that employ large numbers of part-timers. Also, Tilly (1991) maintains that during the 1970s, large numbers of jobs within all industries were absorbed into the secondary labor market. These changes have swelled the ranks of part-time workers even though the work force's desire for part-time jobs has not kept pace, resulting in the growth of involuntary part-time employment.

Several reasons may account for these changes toward more secondary market jobs. First, some companies have simply encountered scheduling difficulties that could be solved most efficiently by using short-hours employees. Second, companies have hired part-time workers as a union busting device. And finally, companies have shifted because they have decided cutting labor costs and enhancing staffing flexibility are more important, at least in some areas of work, than maintaining a stable labor force (Tilly, 1991).

Low-Income Full-Time Workers

Klein and Rones (1989) define the working poor as persons who have devoted at least half the year to labor market efforts, being either employed or in search of a job during that period, but who still lived in poor families. A family of n members is classified as poor if the family income falls below the corresponding poverty threshold for families having n members. Such a poverty threshold is determined by the Government.

With this definition of poverty, Klein and Rones (1989) find that two-thirds of poor full-time workers experienced low earnings, i.e., these workers are poor because their annual earnings are not high enough to take their families above the official poverty threshold. The low-wage level chosen for this analysis is an average of the minimum-wage levels in effect from 1967 to 1987, calculated from each year's value, expressed in 1987 dollars. Furthermore, even among the poor full-time wage and salary workers who also experienced either unemployment or involuntary part-time work, most had earnings below the low-wage threshold defined above (Klein and Rones, 1989). Therefore, underemployment is closely related to poverty.

Overall, a full-time wage and salary worker with earnings below the poverty threshold, had a 25 percent probability of being poor. By comparison, full-time workers who earned more than the low earnings level had only a 2 percent chance of being below the poverty level

(Klein and Rones, 1989). The group most affected by low wages was women heading families containing children. Three-fourths of these women who worked full-time at low wages were living below the poverty level (Klein and Rones, 1989).

Education has been found to have a powerful effect on poverty chances. In 1987, the percentage of poor people with fewer than 4 years of high school was found to be much higher than the percentage poor with 4 years of high school only (13.3 versus 5.7), while the percentage poor with 4 years of college or more was 1.7 (Klein and Rones, 1989).

During the same year, the percentage of poor black males was 10.5, against 4.7 for white males. Black poor females amounted to 16 percent compared to 4.8 percent for white females in the same year. De Anda (1991) analyzed CPS data to find that in 1987 12.2 percent of Mexican male workers 25-34 years old were low-wage earners (below 1.25 times the official poverty threshold), compared to 5 percent of white males in the same age cohort. On the other hand, 19.1 percent of Mexican women in the 25-34 year old cohort earned low wages, while their white counterpart amounted to 12.2 percent. Thus, underemployment is heavily related to race and ethnicity. The case of underemployment and gender is particularly clear for black females.

Families headed by black women are overrepresented among the underemployed, not because black women's earnings are that much lower than white women's, but because such a large proportion of these women are the sole earners in their families (Klein and Rones, 1989). The proportion of all black families headed by women (no spouse present) has risen dramatically over the past several decades, from less than 20 percent in 1950 to more than 40 percent in the 1980s (Wilson and Neckerman, 1986). Part of the rise stems from a dramatic increase over this period in the proportion of never-married black women who head families. Also, black women have much higher separation and divorce rates than white women, and the differences are exaggerated by the very low remarriage rates among blacks (Wilson and Neckerman, 1986).

Age is also another determinant of underemployment by low wages. A large proportion of individuals between 16 to 24 years old are living alone or with unrelated individuals. They generally work at low wages, and, while they have no family to support, neither can they depend on the earnings of other family members to keep them out of poverty (Klein and Rones, 1989).

Taking the median annual earnings for all year-round full-time workers age 16 or over in 1973 as the reference point to determine when a worker wage is low, Bluestone and Harrison (1988a, 1988b) find that the percentage of low-wage year-round full-time workers decreased between 1963 and 1970, then it remained stable until 1979, and it increased during the 1980s. This is the so-called "U-turn effect" (Bluestone and Harrison, 1988a, 1988b; Hinojosa-Ojeda et al., 1991). Bluestone and Harrison (1988a, 1988b) find effects of individual variables on low wages similar to those authors reviewed above. However, they also report effects of structural variables: (1) Regionally, the most exaggerated pattern of low-wage increase is found in the "deindustrializing" Midwest where unemployment rates have remained high in spite of the recent economic recovery and where high-wage manufacturing employment has declined absolutely. (2) As far as industrial sectors are concerned, they find that manufacturing has undergone the same type of U turn as the service economy (including wholesale and retail trade). (3) Slow productivity growth and the shift of employment out of manufacturing have both played a role in generating the low-wage U turn. And finally, (4) the decline in unionization, the erosion in the real value of the minimum wage, the widespread existence of wage concession bargaining, and the secular shift of capital from directly productive to overtly speculative investment, may also be playing a part in this process.

What can be concluded about the determinants of underemployment out of this review of empirical findings? The research on workers suffering the different forms of underemployment shows that there are two sets of variables that are relevant in all the cases:

(1) Individual characteristics. These refer to attributes that qualify individuals for and affect their actual and perceived performance in their positions within the social structures of production and exchange. Social background, motivation, training, intelligence, experience, and skills are examples of such characteristics.

(2) Positions within social relations of production and exchange. These refer to positions within the relations of production, control and authority over factors of production such as money capital, physical capital, and labor. Occupational positions, industrial sectors and exchange positions are considered. Exchange positions refer to positions within the social relations of exchange among production places, consumers, households, and/or worker organizations.

The presence of these structural variables as determinants of discouragement, unemployment, involuntary part-time work, and low-wage full-time work suggest that the mechanisms advanced by macroeconomic theories of unemployment could be extended to cover other forms of labor force hardship besides unemployment. In order to investigate this possibility, several economic theories are reviewed focusing on underemployment.

THE KEYNESIAN CRITIQUE

Demand deficiency theories are based on the work of Keynes (1936). He maintained that the modern economy did not necessarily find its equilibrium at full employment; it could, however find it with unemployment—the underemployment equilibrium. The principle that supply created its own demand—Say's Law—no longer held. The rejection of this law, followed by the call for government spending to sustain demand, were the essence of what came to be called the Keynesian Revolution. For Keynes, the decisive problem of economics was not how the price of goods was established, nor how income was distributed, but how the level of output and employment was determined (Galbraith, 1987) In the neoclassical view, savings and investments were equal. In Keynes' perspective, while output, employment, and income increased, the marginal propensity to consume decreased. Thus, savings increased and nothing guaranteed that, given certain interests rates, these savings were invested due to diverse levels of liquidity preference among firms and people. The result was a reduction in demand for goods, which in turn reduced employment and income. The recession lasted until savings were reduced faster than investment expenditure.

Keynes departed from the neoclassical practice of focusing on the labor market as the ex ante analytic starting point. In his book, he confronted the analysis of equilibrium output and employment levels from labor demand and supply alone. He contended that every shift in the composition of aggregate demand between wage goods and nonwage goods would cause a change in the labor demand curve. On the other hand, labor supply was very likely to be influenced by many other factors besides the real wage. For instance, workers' utility functions could include as arguments not only their individual money wage but also the relative level of comparable workers' pay (Eatwell, 1983).

The mechanism that reduced demand for goods, and that caused a reduction in employment and income could also increase other kinds of underemployment, such as involuntary part-time work, since some employers may have decided to decrease the number of hours workers were hired, a case that was considered by Keynes (1936).

The answer to Keynes from the ranks of neoclassical economics was twofold. On one hand, some economists extended the neoclassical model to include Keynes' developments as a particular case of a more general neoclassical model (Hicks, 1937, 1957). On the other hand, some other economists, known as structuralists, pointed to cases where underemployment is produced for reasons other than demand deficiency (Killingsworth, 1974; Killingsworth and King, 1977). This polemic is known as the structural controversy.

THE STRUCTURAL UNDEREMPLOYMENT CONTROVERSY

Structural underemployment arises: 1) when changes in the pattern of labor demand cause a mismatch between the skills demanded and supplied in a given area, or 2) when such changes cause an imbalance between the supplies and demands for workers across areas (Hamermesh and Rees, 1988). If wages were completely flexible and if costs of occupational or geographic mobility were low, market adjustments would quickly eliminate this type of underemployment. However, in practice, these conditions may fail to hold, and structural underemployment may result (Ehrenberg and Smith, 1988).

Structural underemployment is a group and sector specific inability to match persons and jobs. This view criticizes demand deficiency theory. There may be no lack of demand; however, there is underemployment, since workers lack the skills or training necessary for those jobs available. Killingsworth (1974) and Killingsworth and King (1977) argue that fiscal and monetary policies alone, as may be suggested by Keynesian policies, are not sufficient to eliminate underemployment. They sustain that policy must become targeted directly toward the retraining of these workers and supplying public service employment. This is particularly important in the case of minority workers, since their unemployment ratio is higher than that of of white workers (De Freitas, 1991).

With the coming of the 1960s several young economists, perturbed by the endemic economic problems of some sectors of the population would look at another old paradigm as a source of ideas: marxism (Cain, 1976).

THE CLASSICAL MARXIST APPROACH TO UNDEREMPLOYMENT

Marx's (1967, 1964) critique was directed against the economic equilibrium posited by the classical economists Smith and Ricardo. His view was that economic institutions, such as trade unions, corporations, the economic manifestations and policies of the state, and class conflict, are all in movement or are a source of movement. According to Marx, the classical economists ignored the distribution of power and its influence in the distribution of income, and failed to give an explanation for economic crisis and monopoly (Galbraith, 1987).

Marx (1967) distinguishes between the lumpenproletariat and the industrial reserve army. The first consists of vagabonds, criminals, prostitutes, etc. The second is formed by: (1) the floating surplus population, produced by technological innovation and rising organic composition of capital, i.e., the increase in the proportion of the investments in durable production goods with respect to the investments in labor, which is localized in the centers of modern industry; (2) the latent surplus population, formed by the agricultural labor on its way to becoming the urban or manufacturing proletariat; (3) the stagnant labor army, an already created and disposable reserve of labor, is localized in the capitalized agricultural sector and in the decaying branches of industry, namely, those sectors in transition from manufacture to machinery, and from handicraft to manufacture; (4) the last category is the paupers. Formed by orphans and pauper children; by the demoralized, ragged, sick, and mutilated workers, who are able to find a job only at the height of the business cycle.

Marx's view of underemployment suggests a segmentation of the economy and of the labor market. This is going to be a key idea that appears in the segmentation perspective that encompasses authors from both sociology and economics. However, marxism is not the only source where the segmentation authors have borrowed from, other schools have contributed with their ideas. The next sections unfolds these ideas.

THE SEGMENTATION PERSPECTIVE

The Institutionalist and Neo-Institutionalist Economists

The segmentation perspective is the convergence point of several theories: the structuralist economists, marxist sociologists and economists, and the institutionalist and the neo-institutionalist economists. The institutionalist economists were prominent from about 1890 to 1930, and the neo-institutionalist economists were relevant in the 1940s and 1950s. They criticized neoclassical economics on the grounds that the modern economy was too complex to follow the neoclassical principles. The growing role of governmental regulation and the increase in unionism and bureaucratic institutions such as corporations and the government, were indicators that free competition and perfect access to information no longer existed. The institutionalists oriented their effort toward the elaboration of emergency anti-recessionary programs in the National Recovery Act (G. C. Means), the Federal Farm Board (J. D. Black, M. L. Wilson, and others), and Roosevelt's Brains Trust (R. G. Tugwell and A. Berle). They were among the first economists in the U.S. to theorize the business cycle (Mitchell, 1927). During the 1950s, the neo-institutionalists continued the criticism against the neoclassical school by pointing out to the existence of independent internal and external labor markets (Dunlop, 1957), the predominance of non-competitive markets of goods (Fisher, 1953), and they came as far as to recommend the integration of the socio-political context into economics (Chamberlain, 1969).

Some students of neo-institutionalist economists elaborated the dual labor market theory.

The Dual Economy and The Dual Labor Market

The first stage in the segmentation perspective was Economic Dualism. The motivation for the appearance of this approach comes from the social problems of the 1960s: the persistence of poverty, the continuation of racial and gender inequalities during a time of expanding education and training programs, and the perceived deterioration of the work ethic linked to higher levels of job dissatisfaction (Cain, 1976; Kaufman, 1982).

Averitt (1988, 1968), Reich et al. (1973), and Edwards (1979), distinguish two main economic aggregates in the demand side, alternatively called "center" and "periphery", or "primary" and "secondary" sectors. Averitt (1968, p. 7) defines these economies as the center and the periphery as follows:

> "The new economy is composed of firms large in size and influence. Its organizations are corporate and bureaucratic; its production processes are vertically integrated through ownership and control of critical raw material suppliers and product distributors; its activities are diversified into many industries, regions, and nations."."..[F]irms in the large economy serve national and international markets, using technologically progressive systems of production and distribution."..."We shall call this network of firms the 'center'. The other economy is populated by relatively small firms. These enterprises are the ones usually dominated by a single individual or family. The firm's sales are realized in restricted markets... Let us designate the firms in the small economy by the term 'periphery'".

O'Connor (1973) includes the state as a third sector, comprised of state contracted economic activity and direct state production. He stresses the different relationship between each sector and the state.

The origin of the dual economy is placed by several authors (O'Connor, 1973; Reich et al., 1973; Edwards, 1979), borrowing from Marx, in the capitalist dynamic of concentration and centralization. In this view, capitalists are able to accumulate capital through the extraction of surplus value from labor and from competition among themselves. Centralization occurs because during the periodic economic crisis many businesses fail and are acquired by other capitalists. Thus, center firms are associated with monopoly capitalism, and periphery firms with the remaining small competitive firms.

According to economic dualism, the labor market is divided in two parts: a primary labor market and a secondary labor market. This distinction is placed according to the degree of employment stability (O'Connor, 1973; Doeringer and Piore, 1971). Core firms have implicit contracts, unions, internal labor markets, etc., that decrease turnover and give workers higher levels of benefits: job security, better possibilities for continuing their training, access to job ladders, and lower odds of being laid off. Periphery firms, on the other hand, operate within the external labor market, where there are no barriers to movement into or out of positions (Doeringer and Piore, 1971).

Thurow (1975) has argued that we can think of entry into the primary labor market as being governed by a queue. Workers are ordered according to their costs of trainability. Those workers that start their work experience in the secondary labor market will have unstable labor histories by the nature of their jobs in that sector, and it will be very unlikely for them to move to the primary labor market. This explains the persistence of poverty among some segments of the population, namely, minorities and women (Bluestone, 1970; Gordon, 1972). Following this, Gordon (1972) maintains that due to geographic constraints, only peripheral jobs are available to ghetto minorities. In addition, economic dualism borrows the notion of "taste discrimination" (Becker, 1971) from neoclassical economics to sustain that many employers have a preference for certain workers. However, they argue that only core employers can afford to discriminate, affecting negatively the opportunities of minorities to get good jobs. On the other hand, dualism also argues that employers become engaged in "statistical discrimination" (Beck et al., 1978; Thurow, 1975; Doeringer and Piore, 1971), using minority status, education, and other credentials as inexpensive indicators of trainability.

The picture of underemployment that emerges from this analysis is quite at variance with either the keynesian or the neoclassical conceptions. Whereas the former views most underemployment as involuntary, Doeringer and Piore (1971) argue that this is only true of workers in the primary market. Most underemployment is concentrated in the secondary sector and reflects, not a shortage of vacancies, but the often voluntary turnover of highly mobile workers. Thus, as in the case of neoclassical theory, underemployment is mostly frictional. However, it is concentrated in the secondary labor market. Like in keynesian theory, the primary labor market suffers underemployment only during the recessionary periods. Substantial reductions in underemployment are thus viewed as impossible without interventionist policies by government aimed at improving the quality of secondary employment and accelerating the transition from the secondary to the primary sector (Doeringer and Piore, 1971).

Economic dualism is the main pillar of neo-structuralism. This does not stop the latter from being critical of the former and trying to correct its deficiencies.

Neo-Structuralism and the Determination of Underemployment

Contrary to economic dualism, neo-structuralists recognize the existence of more than two economic sectors (Hodson and Kaufman, 1982). Aside from capital concentration, other dimensions of industrial structure should be considered, such as internal production factors, technical factors of production, and market factors (Hodson, 1983, 1984). Using these dimensions, cluster analyses of industrial data are performed and a number of industrial sectors are identified. Kaufman, Hodson, and Fligstein (1981), and Hodson (1983) identify sixteen clusters, which are later aggregated into six by Hodson (1983). These sectors are: oligopoly, core, periphery, core utilities, periphery utilities, and trades. Schervish (1983), following a different empirical procedure, recognizes seven sectors, including the state as one of them.

Neo-structuralist authors are also critical of neoclassical economics, and particularly of human capital theory's neglect of the possibility that labor outcomes generating processes may vary across different structural contexts. In economic terms, human capital theory concentrates on individual workers' characteristics—the supply side—and ignores the structure of jobs (Fligstein et al., 1983) and the matching process between jobs and individuals—the demand side (Granovetter, 1981). The neo-structuralists believe that structural factors, like firms, jobs and occupations, social classes, unions, and industries not only complement individual factors as determinants of labor outcomes, but they also emphasize that structural factors shape or mediate effects of individual level attributes upon income, underemployment, job satisfaction, etc. (Hodson, 1983; Schervish, 1983; Fligstein et al., 1983; De Anda, 1991). Thus, social rewards are thought of as attributes of positions within the social structure that are determined by structural processes. These processes operate independently of those that allocate individuals among positions (Fligstein et al., 1983).

According to neo-structuralist authors, people receive the rewards they do because of the positions they occupy and, in particular, the power associated with the positions (Schervish, 1983). Favored positions enable incumbents to obtain higher rewards than comparably qualified individuals in less favored positions. Consequently, workers are differently sheltered from underemployment depending upon their personal characteristics, social class, industrial sector, stage of the business cycle, and union membership (Schervish, 1983; Hodson, 1983). However, from this perspective, workers are not seen as passive recipients of the effects of employers' investments or central strategies. On the contrary, economic organization and labor markets can be conceived as offering certain resources and creating certain vulnerabilities for workers (Hodson, 1984, 1983). Higher rewards are not given as a mechanism of social control but are conceded in response to demands from workers because costs can be passed on to customers (Hodson and Kaufman, 1982). On one hand, large firms have the resources to manipulate the environment in which they operate in order to maximize profits (Bluestone and Harrison, 1980). On the other hand, workers in large firms have greater possibilities for communication and organization than workers dispersed in a multitude of small shops (Hodson and Kaufman, 1982).

Although neo-structuralist writers are particularly critical of human capital theory, their criticism of neoclassical economics is more extensive. As Smith (1990) points out, neo-structuralists argue that neoclassical analyses are flawed because:

First, neoclassical analyses are not supported by evidence (Kalleberg and Sorensen, 1979. p. 352). The link stated by neoclassical economists between education and productivity has more to do with credentialism (Berg, 1970; Collins, 1980). Experience, on the other hand, has been reinterpreted as a measure of power rather than skill, since experience could be an indicator of the potential for collective organization of workers, or it could be linked to the bargaining power attached to the possibility of quitting (Kalleberg, Wallace, and Althauser, 1981; pp. 658-9).

Second, the assumptions made by neoclassical economics, namely labor market homogeneity and perfect competition are unreasonable (Kalleberg, 1988, p. 212; Bibb and Form, 1977, p. 975). Workers' situation in the labor market differs across different sectors of the economy, and this makes wages and underemployment vary as well (Bibb and Form, 1977, p. 976).

Third, although economists recognize that discrimination and shelters from competition are an obstacle to equalization of wages and other underemployment chances, they treat them as "market imperfections" (Colbjornsen, 1986, pp. 46-8). This treatment, neo-structuralist writers claim, makes neoclassical theory unfalsifiable and provides an escape for any inconsistency between theory and observations.

Fourth, a serious deficiency of neoclassical economic theories is that they neglect power (Bibb and Form, 1977, p. 976; Kalleberg, 1989, p. 589). Economic theories that assume atomistic individuals are inadequate because they do not consider that effective power rests largely in collective organizations and plays a very important role in determining wages and underemployment likelihood of workers.

Fifth, workers are insulated from external competition by internal labor markets (Sorensen, 1983). Such employment arrangements are produced by the exercise of worker power (Hodson and Kaufman, 1982; p. 730). This means that economic assumptions that wages and underemployment are determined by competitive selection rather than worker power are wrong. Internal labor markets break the link between marginal productivity, earnings, and underemployment likelihood (Sorensen, 1983; pp. 272-8).

Are these criticisms fair? They have been examined by writers both in sociology and economics. Their discussion is presented in the next section.

The Neo-Structuralist Critique. Does It Stand?

The underlying assumption of human capital theory is that worker outcomes, earnings and underemployment are associated with individual productivity, which, in turn, depends on individual capacities. This is relevant, because not all marketable capacities originate in education and training. Some unexplained variance in earnings and underemployment may be accounted for by individual ability or other attributes, like good health (Smith, 1990). Thus, education and training, the most used proxies for measuring human capital variables may not be able to tap all other relevant personal characteristics that influence productivity.

Therefore, education may result to be a mediocre indicator of individual capacities. The reason for this is that the quality of schools varies widely, and much relevant training goes on within the family (Smith, 1990). Also, education may affect personal productivity through its impact on personality in general and work habits in particular and not only by affecting cognition (Bowles and Gintis, 1976; Smith, 1990).

All this means that by showing a weak effect of education on earnings or underemployment, one does not get rid of individual ability in the earnings or underemployment determination processes.

Similarly, the difference across economic sectors in wages and underemployment is perfectly compatible with neoclassical economics, since these differences could be explained by the interaction of supply and demand. Smith (1990; p. 832) argues that differences in the rate of return to human capital between industries or classes that show up in a one-shot cross-sectional study may be accounted for by differences in worker quality or working conditions.

Even Becker (1975; p. 36) recognizes and analyzes barriers to the equalization of rates of return to human capital between industries. These barriers are occupation-specific skill and significant moving expenses. It is not true, then, that all neoclassical economists assume labor market homogeneity. However, it is the persistent differential rates of return to human capital that is at issue. If this is not the case, then orthodox neoclassical analyses are right. However, there is some evidence (Tigges, 1987, 1988) that there are some rates of return advantages to human capital in the core. This could be due to differential capacities to make profits on the basis of exchange advantages (Fligstein, Hicks, and Morgan, 1983; p. 297) or the organizational power of occupational groups (Bibb and Form, 1977; p. 978). On the other hand, there is a standard neoclassical answer to persistent inter-industry differences in rates of return to human capital for earnings and underemployment. It is that unmeasured differences in working conditions and worker quality account for them (Murphy and Topel, 1987). As Smith (1990; p. 831) notes, "the point is that neo-structuralist research has not assembled any data that can allow the worker quality/working conditions hypothesis to be rejected. The new-structuralist research has done nothing useful to settle this issue."

What about market imperfections and falsifiability? Oligopolistic industrial organization may also affect earnings and underemployment, although the economic mechanism is not so obvious. It could be that, as Fligstein et al. (1983) argue, employers use monopoly or oligopoly profits to hire better quality labor. However, this does not explain any wage premiums or underemployment differences due to monopoly or oligopoly, since more productive labor has a lower underemployment likelihood and it increases profits (Smith, 1990), an argument that is consistent with neoclassical economics.

Employers may use their privileged position and discriminate, constituting another market imperfection that increases the probability of underemployment and low wages for minorities and women. But this argument has respectable antecedents in neoclassical literature (Cain, 1976). As a matter of fact, neo-structuralists borrow the discrimination explanations advanced by the neoclassical school, i.e., "taste" discrimination (Becker, 1964), and "statistical" discrimination (Arrow, 1972), as explanations of possible causes of labor inequality (Smith, 1990; Cain, 1976). Union effects on income and underemployment are similarly compatible with orthodox economics (unions restrict the supply of labor) and have played a central role in the work of some economists (Freeman and Medoff, 1984).

Green (1990; Chapters 3, 6, and 9) reviews the literature concerned with various forms of imperfect competition, such as number of firms, barriers to entry, government regulation, technical efficiency, and market power. What all this means is that economists are not evading falsifiability, since they are the ones testing for the possible violations of the orthodox neoclassical assumptions. In the economic literature, both theoretical and empirical analyses of the effects of market imperfections abound.

Does the former discussion include internal labor markets? The main argument, as was commented on above, is that internal labor markets break the connection between marginal productivity, earnings, and underemployment. Internal labor markets are efficient for several reasons:

First, employers may be interested in reducing turnover and providing employment security to reduce worker resistance to train other workers (Doeringer and Piore, 1971). Second, difficulties in monitoring worker performance or malfeasance provide another reason (Lazear and Rosen, 1981).

Therefore, internal labor markets can be explained as the outcome of competitive processes and of worker power. "The extent to which internal labor markets are the creation of power or efficiency is an empirical question that has not been answered by new structuralist research."(Smith, 1990; p. 833). On the other hand, the link between marginal productivity and underemployment or earnings may not be jeopardized. Based on the idea of implicit contracts (Azariadis, 1975) between employers and employees, Farkas and England (1985; p. 128) argue that within any worker cohort, "a typical implicit contract contains a trajectory in which compensation and protection from unemployment increase steadily over the life cycle. This implies that implicit contracts pay employees less than their marginal revenue product in the later years, but their approximate marginal revenue product over the life cycle for those who stay with the firm.". According to this argument, internal labor markets can be reconciled with orthodox economics and there is no single time period over which earnings must equal marginal productivity (Smith, 1990; p. 833).

After this brief review of neo-structuralist critiques of neoclassical economics it seems that it is neo-structuralism that stands in trouble. Consider the measures of power for which earnings and underemployment effects have been established.

These measures comprise: occupational licensure, unions' effects on income and underemployment, seniority, and gender and race-ethnicity differences. The claim is that occupational licensure distorts the operation of markets. However, to state that restrictions in the supply of labor increases its price and decreases labor vulnerability is an old neoclassical topic (Friedman, 1962).

As was commented on before, unions' effects on earnings and underemployment have been also part of the most orthodox neoclassical writings (Freeman and Medoff, 1984; Ehrenberg and Smith, 1991).

With respect to seniority, or the claim that workers get organizationally specific power by accumulating tenure with a specific employer (Kalleberg et al., 1981), one could consider that seniority is a clear human capital measure, and worker bargaining power is linked to the threat of quitting, related to the productivity of the experienced worker (Smith, 1990; p. 835).

The differences between minorities, women, and white men's income and underemployment, theoretically, as was pointed out above, rests on neoclassical theories of discrimination. The empirical finding that minorities, including women, are better off if they are in jobs exposed to competition (Baron and Newman, 1990), is not new for economists (Ehrenberg and Smith, 1991; Hamermesh and Rees, 1988), only reaffirms what economic liberals have said a long time ago (Friedman, 1962).

Summarizing, the neo-structuralist critics of neoclassical economics lack both theoretical substance and empirical support, resting on hypothetical mechanisms that have not been tested accurately, and for most of their conclusions, they only reaffirm what neoclassical economists have known for a long time. Secondly, neo-structuralist writings ignore the recent work in labor economics that relaxes the assumptions of the orthodoxy. These recent economic developments may offer alternative mechanisms to explain the presence of structural effects to those advanced by neo-structuralist writers. The next section develops an application of some of these theories to explain underemployment.

EFFICIENCY WAGE THEORIES AND UNDEREMPLOYMENT

Efficiency-wage theories try to answer several puzzles that have worried economists for decades. One of these puzzles is the persistence of interfirm wage and job differentials (Averitt, 1968; Krueger and Summers, 1987, 1988; Thaler, 1989). A second puzzle is why firms do not decrease wages in order to hire more labor if labor supply increases, particularly during recessions (Yellen, 1984; Katz, 1986). A third one is why do not employers increase productivity standards if workers outdo the current ones, and why unproductive workers are not fired even in cases where employers have detected them (Akerlof, 1982,1984). A fourth puzzle is provided by Tilly (1991), who tests the hypothesis that larger full-time/part-time differentials in wages or fringe benefits would induce employers to hire more part-time workers. However, this hypothesis is not supported by his data analysis. On the contrary, he finds evidence that the effects of the wage and fringe benefits differentials on the ratio of part-time/full-time workers hired are negative. Tilly declares this a puzzling finding.

A possible solution for these puzzles rests on the application of the efficiency-wage theories to jobs. This application may also provide another explanation for underemployment, since the former puzzles involve questions that can be phrased in terms of the differences in the incidence of underemployment and its determinants. In order to account for the high diversity of jobs across firms, the idea is that a firm production function depends on the type of jobs the firm offers to workers, part-time/full-time, as well as the level of wages its workers are paid. Yellen (1984) presents the following rudimentary model that shows the essence of the efficiency-wage models' idea:

$$Q=F(\ e(w)N\ );\ e'(w) > 0,\ \text{and}\ e(0) < 0, \tag{1.1}$$

where Q is the firm's production function, N is the number of employees, e is the effort per worker, w is the real wage at the firm, and e' is the first derivative.

The important feature of model (1.1) is that the firm productivity depends on the wage level. Thus, depending upon the firm production function, each firm optimizes its product by giving a certain wage that may differ from the optimal wage of other firms. This may explain the diversity of wages within or between industrial sectors. Using Yellen's model, we can argue that the firm production function (1.1) may also be a function of the kind of job that employees hold. Therefore, we have the following model of the firm's productivity:

$$Q=F(e(w,J)N);\ D1:e(w,J) > 0;\ e(0,J) < 0;\ e(w,0) < e(w,1),\ \text{for all}\ w, \tag{1.2}$$

where J indicates the type of job the employee holds. J equals 1 if the employee works full-time, otherwise J equals 0. D1 indicates the partial derivative with respect to the first variable, w. Thus, in this model, the amount of effort that workers invest in production depends upon the type of job they have at the firm, or, in other words, of how underemployed they are in the firm. Full-time workers are more productive than part-time workers, because, according to model (1.2), full-timers invest more effort at the firm than part-timers.

According to model (1.2), firms would differ in the distribution of underemployment, since they would hire workers depending upon their particular production functions. Therefore, following this model, it is hypothesized that the likelihood of workers' underemployment may vary across firms and industries, since some firms would hire part-time or low-wage workers, others would hire full-time well-paid workers, while still others would hire fairly-paid part-time workers.

Why should labor productivity depend on wages and the number of hours, i.e., why are full-time or part-time workers hired to work for the firm? Efficiency-wage theories (Yellen, 1984; Akerlof, 1982,1984; Katz, 1986) give an answer for the case of wages. Their argument could be generalized for the case of jobs. Yellen (1984), Katz (1986), and England (1992) summarize various reasons for efficiency-wage contracts:

First, rarely can employment contracts rigidly specify all aspects of a worker's performance. This uncertainty provides the firm with a good reason for the payment of a wage in excess to the worker, as an incentive to work rather than shirk. A similar argument is advanced by Hodson and Kaufman (1982) and Hodson (1984). In the same vein, to provide workers with full-time jobs can constitute a powerful deterrent to shirk. Workers who shirk have some chance of getting caught, with the penalty of being fired. If there is a cost to being fired, the threat of being sacked if caught cheating creates an incentive not to shirk, if the worker makes more with the current employer than s/he could make elsewhere.

The second reason is that firms may also offer wages in excess of market clearing to reduce costly labor turnover. Together with higher wages, firms may also offer full-time jobs. Under these conditions, workers might be more reluctant to quit.

Adverse selection gives the third reason for a relation between productivity, wages, and underemployment. If ability, workers' reservation wages, and workers' full-time employment are positively correlated, firms with higher wages and full-time jobs will attract more able job candidates. The willingness of an individual to work for less than the going wage, or in a part-time job, sets an upper bound on his/her ability, raising the firm's estimate that he/she is a mediocre worker.

Dickens (1986) presents a fourth reason for an efficiency-wage model. It is the threat of unionization. Nonunionized firms that face a threat of unionization pay union or near-union wages and offer full-time jobs in order to avoid unionization.

The fifth reason is due to Akerlof (1982,1984), who provides the first explicitly sociological model leading to the efficiency-wage hypothesis. Akerlof argues that each worker's effort depends on the work norms of his group. Akerlof's partial gift exchange model tries to explain phenomena which seems inexplicable in neoclassical terms: why firms do not fire workers who turn out to be less productive, why piece rates are avoided even when feasible, and why firms set work standards exceeded by most workers. He argues that the firm can succeed in raising group norms and average effort by paying workers a gift of wages in excess of the minimum required, in return for their gift of effort above the minimum required. Along with higher wages, the firm may be successful at raising workers' effort by offering them better jobs.

Akerlof's (1982,1984) model differs from the other efficiency-wage models, since it is not assuming entirely selfish actors, but assuming some norms of altruism and fairness affecting group morale among both employers and employees (England, 1992). Workers' norms of fairness may include the notion that firms should pay higher wages or offer full-time jobs when they have a greater ability to pay, particularly if they have higher profit levels. This may explain why industries' profit rates affect wages and jobs, in contrast to the orthodox claim. "Orthodox theory implies that investment in less-profitable sectors will eventually cease and the sectors will disappear unless their return on investments equals other sectors, and thus that economic profit rates between industries should not differ in the long run." (England, 1992; p. 86).

Efficiency-wage models generalized as in model (1.2) provide one possible explanation for persistent interfirm and interindustry wage and job type differentials. According to England (1992; p.86), efficiency-wage theory also provides a possible explanation for interoccupational wage differentials. A very simple mathematical expression of this case is the following model:

$$Q=F(e1(w1)N1, e2(w2)N2,..., ek(wk)Nk);$$
$$ei'(wi) > 0; ei(0) < 0, i=1,2,...,k, \qquad (1.3)$$

where ei is the effort function of occupation i, wi is the real wage of the ith occupation, Ni is the number of workers in the ith occupation, and ei' is the derivative of the ith effort function. Thus, according to this model, the higher the real wage the higher the effort in every occupation. Model (1.3) also implies different wages across occupations and firms depending upon the firm productivity function.

Model (1.3) is just an efficiency-wage model that can be generalized to an efficiency-wage and job model. The way to do this is by following the same idea as when model (1.2) generalized model (1.1):

$$Q=F(e1(w1,J)N1, e2(w2,J)N2,...,ek(wk,J)Nk);$$
$$D1:ei(wi,J) > 0; ei(0,J) < 0; ei(wi,0) < ei (wi,1);$$
$$J=0,1; i=1,...,k, \qquad (1.4)$$

In model (1.4), ei is the effort function of occupation i, wi is the real wage of the ith occupation, J is a dummy variable that indicates a full-time job ($J=1$), or a part-time job ($J=0$), D1 indicates the partial derivative with respect to the first variable, and Ni indicates the number of workers within the ith occupation. In model (1.4) the effort of workers varies across occupations as in model (1.3), but now workers' effort also depends on the kind of job the worker in that occupation holds. The effort is greater if in the same occupation a worker has a full-time job than if a similar worker holds a part-time job. Thus, model (1.4) implies that wages and jobs (full-time versus part-time) may vary across occupations, firms, and industries. In other words, underemployment is, according to model (1.4), unequally distributed across firms, occupations, and industries.

The integration of human capital variables within the efficiency-wage and job models has to be done carefully. It is not acceptable to assume that workers' effort depends upon the wage, the job type, and workers' investments on education, on-the-job training, and migration, since it has been shown that workers' returns to human capital investments vary across occupations (Wright, 1979). What effect in the firm productivity would a blue collar mining worker have with a college degree? It could have a negative effect, due to high amounts of education decreasing the level of job satisfaction in low-skill jobs (Berg, 1970; Burris, 1983; Rumberger, 1986). Thus, effort does not necessarily increase with education. However, within occupations, there can be a range of educational variation that can increase productivity. Therefore, an increase in higher education may not do any good in low-skill occupations, but it might increase productivity among managers and professionals. Expressed in model form:

$$Q= F[e1(w1,J1,h1)N1,...,ek(wk,Jk,hk)Nk]; \quad D1:ei(wi,Ji,hi) > 0;$$
$$ei(wi,0,hi) < ei(wi,1,hi); \quad ei(0,Ji,hi) < 0; \quad D3:ei(wi,Ji,hi) > 0;$$
$$LLi < hi < ULi; \quad Ji=0,1; \quad i=1,...,k, \tag{1.5}$$

The distinguishing feature of model (1.5) relative to the former ones is the introduction of h, a human capital variable, e.g. education. Similarly, more human capital variables could be introduced. For the sake of simplicity, only one variable is introduced in model (1.5). Education is supposed to increase effort when it is within a certain range of values, different for every occupation, where LLi stands for the lower limit and ULi for the upper limit, relative to the ith occupation. An implication of this model is that the likelihood of underemployment varies depending upon the level of human capital investments across occupational categories. Or, in other words, there exist interactions between occupation and human capital variables over the likelihood of underemployment.

In sum, efficiency-wage models offer the possibility of integrating individual human capital and structural determinants of underemployment. The way this is possible is by considering that the firm production function is influenced by the wage, the kind of job, and by human capital variables, since all these variables affect the effort workers invest in the production process, effort that may vary across occupations. In the following section, some critiques of efficiency-wage theories are considered. Such discussion includes the way efficiency-wage theories try to explain wage and underemployment differences for minorities and women.

Efficiency-Wage Theories: Some Critiques

As was observed above, firms pay efficiency wages in order to increase worker productivity by motivating the desired behavior in the firm workers. This is the core of efficiency-wage theories. Therefore, if employers can find cheaper alternative ways of obtaining the productivity levels than they would achieve by paying efficiency wages, this would invalidate efficiency-wage theories.

One alternative that employers have is the organization of internal labor markets with internal promotions ladders (Doeringer and Piore, 1971) or by using implicit contracts between employers and employees (England, 1992), in which early low wages and high later wages motivate the behavior efficiency-wage models are trying to induce.

Internal labor markets and implicit contracts may work in the primary sector of the economy (Averitt, 1968, 1988; Katz, 1986). The secondary sector, on the other hand, may still pay efficiency wages or else use unemployment as an incentive device (Katz, 1986). However, this is inconsistent with generally higher wages in the core (Katz, 1986). Overcoming this contradiction, Weiss (1990) has pointed to several problems with these critiques of efficiency wage models. First, assigning workers to initial low wage jobs, even if effort were not monitored, is not valid if firms are trying to improve the quality of their labor force or the fitness of their workers. Thus, such a critique does not apply to the adverse selection or nutrition efficiency wage models. Second, making workers accept low initial wages does not motivate them to contribute any effort to the firm. Furthermore, workers with low wages are indifferent between working and staying home, opting for unemployment, if the periods of low wages are long.

Unemployment can potentially be eliminated as a disciplinary threat if workers post performance bonds at the time of hiring that will be forfeited if they are caught shirking, or if they quit or become unionized (England, 1992; Katz, 1986).

Katz (1986) remarks that the bonding schemes have serious problems to be implemented. First, workers, specially young ones, may face capital market constraints and lack of liquidity to post large bonds. Bank financing of performance bonds would be unlikely to be obtained by workers, due to the possibility of personal bankruptcy (Weiss, 1990). Second, firms have an incentive to falsely claim that workers are shirking and claim the bonds. "The difficulty of potential workers in verifying the honesty of a firm's behavior means that the reputation mechanism is quite fragile and may be a far from perfect enforcement mechanism." (p.15).

A possible way out of this problem is the organization of tournament schemes or performance bonds that may permit the firm to commit itself to a wage plan that creates the proper incentives for workers (Katz, 1986; Malcolmson, 1984). However, if all firms were offering straight-time contracts, a deviating firm offering a tournament may not be able to attract any employed workers. Uncertainty concerning which workers will apply to the tournament firm would deter applications from risk averse workers. This situation would bias the pool of applicants toward the unemployed or the low ability types. Therefore, firms are not likely to offer tournament wage schedules (Weiss, 1990).

A number of explanations consistent with standard competitive labor market models are possible for the large impact of industry affiliations on wages and job types even after controlling for measured human capital variables. First, differences in technology across industries make it profitable to hire higher quality workers and therefore pay higher wages and assign full-time jobs in some industries. Second, it is possible that industry wage and job differentials are compensating differentials for nonwage attributes that directly affect the utility of workers. Third, industry wage or job premiums observed at any point in time may only reflect transitory differentials created by shifts in labor demand across sectors and maintained by incomplete labor mobility in the short run. Finally, a fourth possibility is that industry wage and job type differences arise from differences in patterns of human capital accumulation across industries.

The former critiques apply to all the efficiency-wage models based on the assumption of rational individual maximizers. As commented above, the bonding critique is weak. With respect to the existence of implicit contracts or internal labor markets as alternatives to efficiency-wage theories, efficiency wage theorists observe that, "as a practical matter, employers cannot set starting wages low enough to pay for the later above-market efficiency wages . . . In the extreme, this might require a negative starting wage! Minimum wage laws and imperfect capital markets on which workers could borrow this bond may explain why such a solution is impractical." (England, 1992; p. 87). Thus, efficiency-wage theories do not recognize the principle, adopted by implicit contract theory (Azariadis, 1975) that workers are paid the marginal revenue product over their working life cycle (England and Farkas, 1986). In this sense, efficiency-wage theories constitute a greater departure from orthodoxy (England, 1992; p. 87).

The critiques of efficiency-wage theories coming from orthodox neoclassical economics have motivated a lot of econometric work in order to test the relevance of human capital variables. Katz (1986; p. 29) supports the idea that if unmeasured ability is highly correlated with observed labor quality variables, such as years of schooling and labor market experience, then unmeasured labor quality cannot provide an explanation for the large estimated industry wage effects. Krueger and Summers (1986) estimate large effects of industry switches on wages. They conclude that workers moving from high to low wage industries appear to experience wage declines and workers moving from low to high wage industries appear to experience wage gains. On the compensating differentials hypothesis, Krueger and Summers (1986) find that the inclusion of 10 working conditions variables in a standard wage equation barely affects the estimated industry wage premiums. Murphy and Topel (1986) find that differences in unemployment risk across industries can account for only a quite small fraction of industry wage differentials. And Katz (1986) reports research that shows the strong stability of industry differentials over time that appears to rule out transitory demand factors as a major component of the explanation of wage differences. Finally, Krueger and Summers (1986) test if industry wage differences arise from differences in patterns of human capital accumulation across industries. They find that industry wage differentials are approximately equal in magnitude and highly correlated for young and older workers. Also, industry wage differentials are quite similar for different tenure groups (Katz, 1986). If economic based efficiency-wage theories have problems dealing with the alternative that the firm can set performance bonds or tournament schemes, sociological based efficiency-wage theories would consider this a case where collective agreements or norms would set the effort level within the firm. Akerlof (1982) illustrates his theory with an example taken from a study done by Burawoy (1979). In this example, a tournament scheme is used by the firm to motivate worker effort.

As stated by Katz (1986), "[m]ost firms pay careful attention to the perceived fairness and consistency of their internal wage structures. Doeringer and Piore (1971) find that firms devote far more resources to and place more weight in their wage policies on job evaluation programs designed to maintain and/or justify their internal wage structures than to market wage surveys utilized to keep wages in line with those of product or labor market competitors." (Katz, 1986; p. 20). Firm profits may be another variable that influences the firm's internal wage structure (Katz, 1986; Fligstein et al., 1983). This may explain why the firm profits are correlated with its employees' wages, since worker morale and loyalty, and consequently productivity, may depend on the extent that the firm shares its rents with its employees.

Efficiency-wage theories have something to say about the differences in underemployment that minority racial and ethnic groups have vis-a-vis whites. This theory also speaks to gender underemployment differences.

Efficiency Wage Theories and Labor Market Discrimination

Efficiency wage models provide several reasons for persistent discrimination by race and sex in a competitive labor market. Underemployment and wage differences may originate in group differences related to productivity.

If two identifiable labor market groups differ in their rates of turnover, quitting, shirking, proclivity to become unionized, or in the quality of their skills, then the group with the higher propensity to one of these choices is likely to require greater inducement not to do it. Bulow and Summers (1986) show that in the dual labor market version of the shirking model that the higher turnover group must be overrepresented in the secondary sector since if the wage is the same for both groups in the primary sector, the shorter horizon group is more likely to shirk unless the chances of being able to get a primary job in the future are lower than for the long horizon group. Poterba and Summers (1984) find a higher rate of labor force withdrawal for women aged 25 to 59 than for men in the same age group, consequently, women will be segregated occupationally and industrially in lower paying or part-time jobs that are easier to monitor. However, England (1992; Chap. 1) disputes this findings. She posits that "the evidence is not clear on whether women's quit rates are higher than men's beyond what can be explained by job placements that result from discrimination (other than merely statistical discrimination)." (p. 88). Similarly, England (1992) disputes that women have higher turnover rates than men, that women are harder to unionize than men, and also argues that there is no reason why firms would prefer a high quality male worker to a high quality female one (p. 89).

Even if there are no real differences in productivity between females and males, or among Latino, African American, and white workers, employers may still perceive (false) productivity differences that lead to statistical discrimination. A taste for discrimination may also lead to different expectations of group differences in productivity that may bias evaluation of job performance (Bielby and Baron, 1986). In particular, workers of lower expected productivity may be given less on-the-job training. As Kirschenman and Neckerman (1991; p. 231) put it for the case of race:

> "[T]he qualities more likely to be proxied by race are not job skills but behavioral and attitudinal attributes—dependability, strong work ethic, and cooperativeness—that are closely tied to interactions among workers and between workers and employers."

Therefore, employers may prefer not to hire workers from a group that is perceived to be more likely to shirk, to quit the job, to be less productive, less dependable, or less cooperative.

England (1992) sees better possibilities to explain gender differences in the gift exchange model (Akerlof, 1982,1984). This model explains gender and ethnic differences in hiring by emphasizing social relations in the workplace. If prevailing norms outside the firm are sexist or racist, these norms are reflected inside the workplace causing divisions among workers (Burawoy, 1979). Such divisions may affect cooperation and decrease productivity within the firm. Worker conflict may alter the norms of gift exchange between the firm and the workers (Akerlof, 1982), affecting the amount of productive effort workers yield to the firm. To avoid conflict, employers may prefer to hire female and minority workers outside of the efficiency wage and job industries, where the norms of gift exchange do not matter. Such solutions make female and minority workers more likely to experience higher underemployment rates.

Akerlof (1984) has pointed out the similarities between efficiency wage theories and the dualistic perspective (Gordon, 1972; Edwards, 1979). As in the case of dualism, efficiency wage theory finds that discrimination occurs within the economic sector(s) that can afford it, the core and the state, in the case of the dualistic approach (Gordon, 1972; O'Connor, 1973), and the efficiency wage sector, in the case of the efficiency wage family of theories (England, 1992). Those workers who cannot obtain jobs in the core, the state, or the efficiency wage sector, will go to the periphery, the sector without efficiency wages, or remain unemployed until they get a job in the core, the state, or the efficiency wage sector. Discrimination could be present both at the entry ports of the core, the state, or the efficiency wage sector, as well as within these economic sectors, as hypothesized by Doeringer and Piore (1971), due to internal job segregation.

Is there any other argument, aside from the ones discussed previously, that could explain differences in underemployment for minority groups and women? Katz (1986) suggests that groups facing capital market restrictions are more likely to be affected by underemployment. "[I]f disadvantaged groups are liquidity constrained and unable to post bonds (accept deferred payment schemes), they will be less able to get primary sector jobs." (p. 43). This may explain why nonwhites are overrepresented relative to whites in secondary sector jobs (Dickens and Lang, 1985). However, this argument draws from a bonding, and not from an efficiency-wage model.

What determines that some groups are more disadvantaged than others? The answer may be a dynamic process that efficiency wage theories of underemployment are not able to tap into. Some sociologists and economists have come up with some answers. Their views look at macroeconomic processes and constitute what is known as the deindustrialization hypothesis.

DEINDUSTRIALIZATION AND
UNDEREMPLOYMENT

Based upon research that Bluestone and Harrison (1980) have done, one could argue that the increase in long term underemployment stems from a structural shift of the economy away from primary sector jobs in manufacturing (Averitt, 1968, 1988). New jobs are being created, but mainly in lower wage sectors, particularly in services (Kasarda, 1983). Bluestone and Harrison (1988) estimate that nearly three fifths of net new jobs created between 1979 and 1984 were low wage, defined as jobs paying below one half the average 1973 real wage. A major reason for this finding is that more than 9 out of 10 of the new jobs created from 1979 to 1984 were part-time or part-year (Nardone, 1986; Shank, 1986; Stinson, 1986). On the other hand, among workers with full-time jobs before being displaced who were reemployed by 1984, nearly 13 percent had found only part-time work and about one half were working in a different industry. Those displaced from manufacturing experienced earnings losses averaging $71 per week (De Freitas, 1991).

The process of deindustrialization has been characterized by accelerated capital mobility across state and national borders, a high volume of permanent layoffs and plant closings in basic industries in the 1970s, downward trends in growth rates of capital formation and research spending, and the dramatic import penetration of American markets for manufacturers (Bluestone and Harrison, 1980). Minority workers have been particularly affected by this process (De Freitas, 1991). Wilson (1980, 1987) identifies deindustrialization as part of the process of formation of the black underclass in the inner cities of the northeastern and midwest regions of the country, the most affected by these structural changes.

Deindustrialization may be related to the flight of industries with efficiency wages or with internal labor markets away from certain areas taking with them high salary and full-time jobs, leaving workers in those areas more vulnerable to underemployment. This suggests that the deindustrialization view is compatible with other underemployment theories.

What then explains underemployment? Based upon the former survey, it is impossible at this point to declare one of the theories an absolute winner. It looks like different theories tap on different aspects of underemployment processes. However, it is possible to reach some conclusions that will help to link this chapter with the empirical work in the next one.

CONCLUSION

Several underemployment theories were analyzed in this chapter. Neoclassical economics (Hamermesh and Rees, 1988), keynesianism (Galbraith, 1987), institutionalism (Dunlop, 1957), neo-structuralism (Fligstein et al., 1983), efficiency-wage theories (Katz, 1986), implicit contract theory (Farkas and England, 1985), and deindustrialization (Bluestone and Harrison, 1980, 1988). Efficiency-wage theories and implicit contract theory are part of the new neoclassical labor economics (England, 1992). All these theories offer plausible mechanisms to explain many underemployment situations. Neoclassical economics, including human capital theory (Becker, 1964), emphasize competition and individual characteristics that increase productivity. Keynesianism looks at demand deficiency. The institutionalists are one of the inspirational sources of neo-structuralism, which admits the importance of structural contextual variables in the explanation of underemployment. Power differentials are the key mechanism used by neo-structuralists to explain differences in underemployment among workers, and power varies across occupations, industries, and ethnic and gender groups.

Efficiency wage theories include economic and sociological theories (Yellen, 1984). They differ in that the economic versions assume rational maximizer individuals, while the sociological version considers the norms and values of groups of workers in the firm. They have in common the assumption that the firm productivity depends on wages. I extended this assumption to include the type of job the worker has in the firm. This extension results in a model that accepts variation in wages and underemployment across firms. The reason for this variation is multiple: firms may experience worker turnover, quits, unionization threats, adverse selection of workers, or diverse group norms of efficiency at work. Such variations may cause discrimination of women and nonwhites, although some authors dispute the evidence on turnover, quit and unionization likelihood between men and women (England, 1992).

Efficiency wage theories offer alternative explanations for the underemployment variation across industries. However, implicit contracts may be an alternative reason for having efficiency wages or jobs. Finally, deindustrialization theory offers a dynamic view of the process of creation of underemployment: Capital flight out of the Midwest and Northeast regions increases the occurrence of underemployment, since many firms that provided good full-time jobs are leaving those areas. The effects are particularly negative for minorities living in the inner cities (Wilson, 1987, 1980).

This chapter has also shown the need to test the mechanisms that the different theories advance. Until this is done, no theory qualifies as being better than the others, since, as was discussed above and summarized in Table 1.1, the same effects of a number of variables on underemployment are hypothesized by various theories through different mechanisms. Chapter 2 will show that the empirical work on underemployment is not free from having problems.

Efficiency wage theories offer alternative explanations for the underemployment variation across industries. However, implicit contracts may be an alternative reason for having efficiency wages or jobs. Finally, deindustrialization theory offers a dynamic view of the process of creation of underemployment: Capital flight out of the Midwest and Northeast regions increases the occurrence of underemployment, since many firms that provided good full-time jobs are leaving those areas. The effects are particularly negative for minorities living in the inner cities (Wilson, 1987, 1980).

This chapter has also shown the need to test the mechanisms that the different theories advance. Until this is done, no theory qualifies as being better than the others, since, as was discussed above and summarized in Table 1.1, the same effects of a number of variables on underemployment are hypothesized by various theories through different mechanisms. Chapter 2 will show that the empirical work on underemployment is not free from having problems.

Table 1.1 Comparison of theories of underemployment.

Variable	Effect on Underemployment	Theory	Mechanism
Age	decreases	h-c	increase in productivity
		n-st	seniority / internal labor markets
		i-c	implicit contracts
Education	decreases	h-c	increase in productivity
		n-st	increase in power / credentialism
Gender	increases for women	n-c/h-c	lower human capital/ discrimination
		n-st	lack of power / discrimination
		e-w	higher turnover or quit rates, less likely to be organized / lack of access to capital markets
Race/ethnicity	increases for nonwhites	n-c/h-c	low human capital / discrimination
		n-st	lack of power / discrimination
		e-w	higher turnover or quit rates / lack of access to capital market
Union membership	decreases	n-c	monopoly effect
		n-st	increase in worker power

Variable	Effect	Theory	Mechanism
Occupation	increases for low status occupations	n-c/h-c	low human capital / demand-supply effects
		n-s	decrease in worker power / difficult to supervise managers and professionals
	varies across occupations	e-w	worker effort and productivity vary across occupations and firms
Industry	increases for retail, trade and services	n-s	variation in profits and worker power / internal labor markets
	no variation	n-c	competition
	varies	e-w	firm productivity varies
	varies	i-c	implicit contracts
	varies	k	variation in demand
Geographic region	increases in Midwest and Northeast	d	deindustrialization / capital flight

Note. The effects of several individual and structural variables are shown with the mechanisms that produce those effects according to the theories.

d = deindustrialization   i-c = implicit contract theory   n-st = neo-structuralism
e-w = efficiency-wage theory   k = keynesian
h-c = human capital theory   n-c = neoclassical theory

Chapter 2

The Modeling of Underemployment

INTRODUCTION

This chapter starts the second objective of this study, the modeling of underemployment in order to investigate the hypothesized effects summarized in Table 1.1. First, the data is introduced, a sample of workers from the 1990 Current Population Survey (CPS). Second, an ordinal logistic regression model is presented followed by a discussion of how such a model fits the ordinal nature of underemployment advanced in the literature (Clogg, 1979; Clogg et al., 1986). Finally, the operationalization of the dependent and the independent variables used in the model is discussed. This particular set of independent variables used in the modeling of underemployment is determined by the theoretical discussion in Chapter 1.

THE DATA

A cross-sectional analysis is performed for the year 1989. The source of data for this study is the March Current Population Survey (Annual Demographic File) for the year 1990. The Current Population Survey (CPS) is a monthly survey conducted by the Bureau of Labor Statistics (BLS) in cooperation with the Census Bureau. The March CPS includes about 70,000 households and represents the noninstitutionalized population of the United States. The interviews followed a multistage cluster sample design and contains about 120,000 persons.

The CPS is an ideal source of data to study labor force outcomes, since it includes items dealing with the demographic characteristics of the population. Data on current employment status, work experience, occupation, industry, and income sources and amounts, are also contained.

The data used in this study includes samples restricted to individuals between the ages of 16 and 64. The term "Mexican origin population" refers to individuals who identified themselves as Mexican American, Chicano, Mexican or Mexicano. The CPS over-samples the Latino population ("Spanish households") since 1976. However, it lacks information to identify the Mexican descent population by country of birth. The samples include all the respondents of Mexican origin who were part of the experienced, civilian labor force during the reference week in which the surveys were conducted.

A number of subsamples from the data source described above are used in the model discussed next. The size of the subsample used in each case is specified in the corresponding report of the estimation of the model in Chapter 3. The next section discusses the modeling of underemployment.

THE MODEL

The adequate model for underemployment depends of the particular nature of that variable, which is a limited dependent variable (Maddala, 1983). This means that the usual regression models are not applicable in this case. Thus, alternative techniques are necessary.

The dependent variable, Economic Underemployment (EU), is considered an ordered polytomous variable (Clogg et al., 1986; p. 389). EU is arranged in a decreasing "order of severity" according to a three dimensional hierarchical criteria: (1) the number of hours the worker has been hired for; (2) the amount of the wage; and (3) the attachment to the labor market (Clogg et al., 1986). The screening of workers proceeds from highest hardship to lowest hardship type of labor force participation, depending upon the EU category they occupy as follows: (1) subunemployment (proxy for discouraged workers); (2) unemployment; (3) involuntary part-time workers; (4) low income full-time workers; and (5) adequately employed full-time workers.

The three dimensional criteria works as follows: First, according to time of participation in the labor market, categories (1) and (2) have the highest hardship, then in a decreasing order category (3) comes next, and finally categories (4) and (5) are at the bottom. In order to distinguish between the levels of hardship confronted by categories (4) and (5), the second dimension, wage, is utilized. Then category (4) precedes (5) in terms of hardship, given that the wage of workers in the former category is smaller than the wage of those workers in the latter. Finally, the third dimension, attachment to the labor market, distinguishes between categories (1) and (2). Discouraged workers in category (1) face a tougher situation in the labor market than unemployed workers in category (2), since discouraged workers are not in the labor market. Although underemployment has been defined as an ordered variable (Clogg et al., 1986), the models used in the literature on underemployment have not used this property. Clogg (1979), and Clogg and Sullivan (1983) used log-linear models without taking the ordering of underemployment into account. DeAnda (1991) utilizes logistic regression models to model a binary dependent variable (underemployed or not underemployed). Therefore, these former approaches are not considering important information about the measurement level of underemployment, since an ordinal variable contains more information than a nominal one. It is because of this hierarchical order of measurement that regression models, which are intended for interval or ratio measurements, cannot be used for underemployment. This is a more serious problem in the binary model mentioned above, since this model is assuming that the independent variables have equal effects on all the different types of underemployment, a case that may not be necessarily true. In fact, this could be a proposition to be tested. Thus, if the ordinality of underemployment is justified, it is appropriate to model underemployment by using a multinomial ordinal model (Maddala, 1983; Agresti, 1990) that is presented next.

A Multinomial Ordinal Model for Underemployment

Let Y_i denote the dependent variable, EU, where $Y_i=j$, if the ith worker is in the jth category stated above, j=1, 2,..., 5. For example, Y2=1 means that the second worker in the sample is in category 1, i.e., this person is a discouraged worker. Thus, the model to be utilized can be expressed as

$$P\{ Yi <= k \mid Xi \} = F(Ak + B'Xi), \qquad (2.1)$$

where the conditional probability that the ith worker is in the kth category or below, given a vector of individual and structural characteristics Xi, is assigned by the cumulative distribution function (cdf) F, evaluated at Ak + B'Xi, being Ak a vector of parameters corresponding to the kth category, and B the vector of coefficients attached to Xi. Vectors Ak and B are the parameters to be estimated in the model. The cdf F is usually assumed to be the logistic or the normal distribution. In the first case, an ordered polytomous logit model is used, while in the second case, an ordered polytomous probit model is in place. In this study, the logistic distribution is assumed, due to the useful interpretation of the results in terms of cumulative logits. However, the difference between the estimates advanced by these two models is not significant, except in the tails of the distribution functions (Hanushek and Jackson, 1977).

Let F be the logistic cdf. Model (2.1) can be written as

$$Lj(Xi)= \ln\{ [P1(Xi)+...+Pj(Xi)]/[Pj+1(Xi)+...+P5(Xi)]\}= Ak$$
$$+B'Xi, j= 1,...,5, \qquad (2.2)$$

where $Pj(Xi)= P\{ Yi= j \mid Xi \}$. $Lj(Xi)$ gives the cumulative logits, understood as the logarithm of the odds of being in category j or below, versus being in category j+1 or above (Agresti, 1990; pp. 321-324).

The vector of independent covariates of the ith individual, Xi, is formed by the individual human capital and demographic characteristics: age, age squared, gender, ethnicity (white, mexican, black), and educational attainment; also included in Xi are the structural and contextual variables: occupation, economic sector, union membership, and geographic region. The estimation of several multinomial ordinal models is presented and discussed in Chapter 3.

Thus far nobody has questioned Clogg et al.'s (1986) assumption of ordinality in the underemployment categories. Is it really valid? Clogg et al. (1986; p. 389) indicate that the hierarchy of underemployment types is due to an "order of severity". Thus, discouraged workers have the highest level of hardship and well paid full-time workers the lowest. The problem with this idea is to operationalize it. Clogg et al. (1986) seem to be using a three dimensional order argument to order underemployment: the number of hours the worker has been hired (full-time or part-time), the wage (above or below certain poverty threshold), and attachment to the market (in or out of the labor force). Thus, according to the number of hours dimension, discouraged workers and unemployed workers have the same hardship level. However, if the third dimension is taken into consideration, unemployed workers are more attached to the market than the discouraged workers. Furthermore, there might be some involuntary part-time workers who receive a higher wage than the low-wage full-time workers, and it is also possible that some involuntary part-time workers receive higher earnings than some fairly paid full-time workers. Thus, the hardship hierarchy argued by Clogg et al. (1986) is questionable. Nevertheless, it still might be possible to justify somehow the ordering of the underemployment components, but in case this assumption is invalid, the modeling of underemployment cannot be done with the ordinal model (2.1) introduced above. An alternative model is necessary, this time without the ordinality assumption.

Operationalization of the Variables

This study follows the definitions and procedures utilized by the Bureau of Labor Statistics (BLS) to count the number of discouraged, as well as the number of unemployed workers (Buss and Redburn, 1988; Hauser, 1972, 1974, 1977). The discouraged workers are those individuals out of the labor force, i.e., those respondents in the CPS survey who did not work during the reference week, and that did not look for work during the previous four weeks, but that want a regular job now, either part- or full- time. The acceptable reasons for not looking for work, in order to be classified as a discouraged worker are: (1) the worker believes no work is available in line of work or area; (2) could not find any work; (3) lacks necessary schooling, training, skills, or experience; (4) believes employers think that he or she is too young or too old; and (5) has other personal handicap in finding a job (e.g., racial discrimination, or a criminal record).

If the respondent provides any other reason besides the ones mentioned above, he or she is excluded from the discouraged worker category.

The official definition of unemployment (U.S. Department of Commerce, 1982; pp. 120-121) includes those non-institutionalized individuals sixteen years and over, who did not have a job during the reference week, were available for work at that time, and (1) were actively seeking employment for the past four weeks; (2) are waiting to be called back to a job from which they had been laid off; or (3) are waiting to report to a new wage or salary job within thirty days. The unemployed includes job leavers, job losers, new job entrants, and job reentrants. A layoff is an individual who is unemployed but expects to be called back to a specific job. If he or she expects to be called back within thirty days, it is considered a temporary layoff; otherwise, it is an indefinite layoff.

Involuntary part-time workers are those who work less than 35 hours per week and would prefer to work full time, but are not working full time as a result of slack work, material shortages or repairs to plant or equipment, new job started during the interview week, job terminated during the interview week, or could only find part-time work.

The low income underemployed workers, or "the working poor", are those workers who work full-time during the reference week, but their annual market-related earnings may not be enough to provide them with adequate income to meet their needs. Clogg and Sullivan (1983) define income inadequacy if the worker's previous year income is below 1.25 times the Poverty Threshold for an individual.

Finally, the adequately employed workers are those individuals that hold full-time jobs, and receive annual market-related earnings above 1.25 times the Poverty Threshold for an individual, during the week of the interview.

Having indicated briefly how to operationalize the dependent variable, the operationalization of the independent variables is developed next.

Previous research has shown that age is a good indicator of workers' experience (Clogg, 1979; Sullivan, 1978), although much better for men than women. Age is used in this study as a continuous-level variable. The information of the respondent's age is reported by the CPS. Education is operationalized as the number of completed years of schooling. The CPS reports of state of residence are used to operationalize geographic region. This study uses the same classification of regions adopted by the CPS (U.S. Department of Commerce, 1990): Northeast, Midwest, West, and South. Table 2.1 shows the distribution of states in these categories. Three dummy variables are used, keeping the Northeast region as the base category.

Table 2.1   Classification of States by Regions.

Region	States
Northeast	Connecticut, Maine, Massachusetts, Vermont, New Hampshire, Rhode Island, New Jersey, New York, Pennsylvania
Midwest	Illinois, Indiana, Michigan, Ohio, Wisconsin, Iowa, Kansas, Minnesota, Missouri, North Dakota, South Dakota, Nebraska
West	Arizona, New Mexico, Colorado, Idaho, Montana, Nevada, Utah, Wyoming, Alaska, California, Hawaii, Oregon, Washington
South	Alabama, Virginia, Kentucky, West Virginia, Mississippi, Tennessee, Arkansas, Louisiana, Oklahoma, Texas, Delaware, District of Columbia, Florida, Georgia, North Carolina, South Carolina, Maryland

Source: Current Population Survey (CPS) 1990

Occupational categories are operationalized following the two-digit code classification system employed by the U.S. Census Bureau, and reported by the CPS for its respondents' (U.S. Department of Commerce, 1990) current or last job. The occupational categories used in the analysis are: (1) executives, administrators, managers, and professionals, (2) technicians, sellers, and administrative support, (3) service, (4) precision production, craft, repair, and operators. Three dummy variables are used to operationalize these categories, taking the fourth category as the base group.

Two different operationalizations of economic sectors are used in separate models. The first operationalization of industrial sectors is based on the two-digit code for industry that the CPS provides for each respondent's current or last job, based on the Census Industry Classification System (U.S. Department of Commerce, 1990). The industry categories used in this analysis are: (1) agriculture, forestry and fisheries, (2) mining, (3) construction, (4) manufacturing, (5) transportation, communications, and other public utilities, (6) wholesale and retail trade, (7) services, and (8) public administration. Seven dummy variables are constructed to operationalize these categories, using public administration as the base industrial sector for comparison.

The second operationalization is based on the three-digit code for industry, but now industries are classified in three categories: Core, State and Periphery, according to the typology advanced by Hodson (1977) and also shown in Beck, Horan, and Tolbert (1978). Two dummy variables are utilized taking the Periphery sector as the baseline. This operationalization is intended to test hypotheses coming from neostructuralists theories of underemployment, while the former operationalization that uses industry types is intended to test hypotheses related to efficiency wage theories.

In sum, the operationalization of underemployment and the independent variables in the ordinal logistic model (2.1) and (2.2) follows standard procedures in the literature. In the section below the whole chapter is summarized.

CONCLUSION

The former literature on underemployment has not considered the ordinality of underemployment as defined by Clogg et al. (1986). If indeed underemployment can be considered ordered, the best model to investigate the effects of the individual and structural variables hypothesized by various theories in Chapter 1 is model (2.2), an ordinal polytomous logistic regression model (Agresti, 1990; Maddala, 1976).

This chapter has been dedicated to discuss the operationalization of the variables used in the model. Several individual and structural independent variables are operationalized: age, education, gender, race, ethnicity, unionization, occupation, industry, and geographic region. The software utilized to run these models is introduced in Chapter 3. There the findings and the estimation of the models are discussed.

Chapter 3

Estimation and Findings

INTRODUCTION

In this chapter the ordinal logistic model for underemployment presented in Chapter 2 is estimated. Several ordinal models test the effects that diverse sets of independent variables produce on underemployment following the guidelines of the theories reviewed above in Chapter 1. A summary of these hypothetical effects can be seen in Table 1.1. In view of these theories, the coefficients of the models are interpreted and discussed.

THE ESTIMATION OF THE ORDINAL POLYTOMOUS MODEL

Several ordinal polytomous models are estimated for various sets of independent variables. The first model of this type is the model shown in Table 3.1. The set of covariates used in this model comes from neoclassical economics/human capital theory and neostructuralism: age, educational attainment, age squared, occupations, and industrial sectors (core and periphery). Controls for ethnicity, gender, and union membership have also been considered.

The negative signs of the variables indicate that being older, having higher educational attainment, being a union member, having an occupation other than blue collar, and being in the core or in the state (relative to the periphery) sectors increases the probability of being in a higher category of underemployment rather than in a lower category. On the other hand, the positive signs of the variables: the square of age, being black, and being a woman does the opposite, that is, increases the probability of being in a lower category rather than in a higher one.

In order to further illustrate the interpretation of the estimated coefficients, let us take education. The negative sign of this coefficient means that education increases the odds of being in a higher category rather than in a lower category, according to model (2.2). Furthermore, the odds ratio indicates that one year increase in education increases the odds of being in a higher category versus being in a lower category 1.1 times (or 1/.90), as Table 3.1 shows. The farther away the odds ratio departs from 1 in any direction, the higher the effect of the variable under consideration. In this study, if the magnitude of the odds ratio is larger (smaller) than or equal to 1.30 (1/1.30), such an odds ratio is considered significantly different from 1. Thus, in the case of education, an odds ratio of 1.1 is not different from 1; therefore, an increase of one year of education does not have a very strong effect on the likelihood of being in a higher category of underemployment rather than in a lower one.

Thus, according to the estimates in Table 3.1, the more a worker invests in human capital (work experience and education), the more likely that worker is to be in a higher underemployment category, i.e., that worker is less likely to be underemployed vis-a-vis a worker with less human capital investments. Therefore, the hypotheses based on human capital theory in Table 1.1 are confirmed by these results. The significance of the structural controls indicates that workers being in the core or in the state economic sectors of the economy are less likely to be underemployed than those workers in the periphery. Similarly, workers in occupations other than blue collar are more likely to be less vulnerable to underemployment than blue collar workers. However, the odds ratio corresponding to service occupations (0.88) indicates that the underemployment likelihood of these workers with respect to the underemployment likelihood of blue collar workers is practically the same, since such an odds ratio is very close to 1. Overall, these results support hypotheses on Table 1.1 based on neostructuralism.

Table 3.2 shows the estimates of an ordinal model that controls for human capital variables and for geographic region. In this model, union membership, ethnicity, gender, industrial sector and occupational controls have been omitted because their inclusion could eliminate the effect of geographic region. Bluestone and Harrison (1988) explain the dissimilarity of workers' situations across geographic regions arguing that black workers are more concentrated in the Midwest, which is also the area of the country suffering the highest rates of deindustrialization in manufacture. Similar to the results in Table 3.1, Table 3.2 shows that human capital variables are significant and in the expected direction, i.e. higher amounts of human capital make workers more likely to be in higher, or more favorable, categories of underemployment. In the case of geographic regions, relative to the Northeast, the baseline region, workers in regions other than the Northeast are more likely to be in lower categories of underemployment rather than in higher ones. However, as it can be observed by examining the odds ratios, such differences among geographic regions are not significant, given that the odds ratios do not depart significantly from 1.

In sum, based on the results from Tables 3.1 and 3.2, human capital/neoclassical economic theory's hypotheses are verified by the ordinal model (2.2). Similarly, neostructuralism is supported by the results shown by these tables. Workers in the periphery seem to be more likely to suffer from underemployment than workers in other economic sectors. On the other hand, deindustrialization theory does not seem to be supported by these results. There are no significant differences in underemployment across geographic regions according to the estimated ordinal model. Thus, the expected disadvantage of the Midwest relative to other regions of the country is not present in Table 3.2.

Table 3.3 shows the estimation of a polytomous ordinal model that includes occupation, union membership, and industrial sector, as structural variables besides the human capital variables. This model is mainly testing the hypotheses based on efficiency wage theories on Table 1.1. Authors writing within this perspective do not accept the operationalization in core and periphery sectors used in the previous version of the model in Table 3.1; rather they use industry types to test their hypotheses (Krueger and Summers, 1988).

An inspection of the estimates in Table 3.3 indicates that the coefficients of the human capital and union membership variables are still significant when the new structural variables are included. And the analysis of the coefficients of the new structural variables gives the following information:

First, all the coefficients of the occupational dummies are significant and negative. This means that, as can be seen in Table 3.3, being a manager or a professional, a technician, a seller, working in administrative support, or in a service occupation increases the probability of being in a higher category of underemployment rather than in a lower category with respect to precision production workers, craft workers, repair workers, and operators, which is the base category.

Second, all the industrial sector coefficients are significant except the ones corresponding to manufacture, transport, communication, and public utilities. The positive sign of the significant coefficients means that with respect to the base industrial sector category, which is the public administration sector, the workers in the other sectors (agriculture, fisheries, mining, construction, wholesale and retail trade, and services) have a higher probability of being in a lower underemployment category rather than in a higher one.

If one looks at the odds ratio reported in Table 3.3 it is possible to gauge the relative importance of the variables to determine underemployment probabilities. In the case of occupations, the odds ratio of service occupations with respect to blue collar occupations is 0.69, i.e. approximately 1. Thus, the effect on the underemployment probabilities if a worker holds a service or a blue collar occupation is approximately the same. However, the odds ratios for managerial and professional occupations (0.216), and for technical occupations (0.376) with respect to blue collar occupations reflect larger differences. That is, workers in professional, managerial, or technical occupations are much more likely than blue collar workers to be in higher underemployment categories.

Several industrial sectors, such as manufacturing, transportation, and public utilities, do not have significant coefficients. This means that the corresponding odds ratios are equal to 1. So, workers in these sectors are as likely to be underemployed as those workers in the public administration sector, the reference category. A very different situation seems to exist in the other sectors. The odds ratios of the services sector (2.612), agriculture, forestry and fisheries (2.888), construction (3.098), mining (1.947), and whole sales and retail trade (2.730), indicate that workers in these sectors have between twice and three times the odds of being in lower categories of underemployment (rather than in higher categories) than do workers in the public administration.

The models estimated in Tables 3.1, 3.2, and 3.3 including structural variables, are consistent with most of the effects hypothesized by the mechanisms of the theories summarized in Table 1.1. High status occupations (professionals, managers, and technicians) have a lower likelihood of being underemployed than low status occupations (services and blue collar) due to differences in unmeasured human capital, demand-supply effects, differences in worker power, or variations in worker effort productivity across occupations and firms. Analogously, underemployment varies across industries because of the existence of internal labor markets, implicit contracts, profit variation, worker effort across firms and industries as hypothesized by efficiency wage theories, or variation in demand.

In sum, the ordinal logistic model supports the hypothesized effects summarized in Table 1.1 relative to neoclassical/human capital and structuralist theories, except in one case: deindustrialization theory is not supported by the results of the ordinal model, since workers of all geographic regions have similar underemployment probabilities. Another exception to the hypotheses supported is related to ethnic group differences. This is discussed next.

The Effect of Ethnicity and Gender on Underemployment

Tables 3.1 and 3.3 show significant effects for blacks and women. Both groups have positive effects with odds ratios that depart from 1 significantly. Thus, black and female workers are more likely to be in lower rather than in higher categories of underemployment vis-a-vis non-black and male workers, respectively.

Given that human capital and structural controls have been already included, the residual effect of being black or female might be due to the presence of different forms of discrimination: taste (Becker, 1971), statistical (Ehrenberg and Smith, 1991), or error (England, 1992).

All the ethnicity and gender coefficients are in the expected direction except for the case of the Mexican ethnicity variable, which in Tables 3.1 and 3.3 indicate that Mexicans are as likely as non-Mexicans, mostly whites, of being equally underemployed. Thus, while all the other coefficients can be explained by following the different mechanisms that the theories in Table 1.1 advance, the case of the Mexican workers constitutes a result that goes against these theories' expectations.

How to explain that Mexicans are as underemployed as non-Mexicans?

Previous studies comparing Mexican and white workers have shown that Mexicans tend to be younger than whites and to have less education than comparable whites in the same cohort (DeFreitas, 1991). Using CPS 1990 data, I find that Mexicans are younger (the age average is 33.42 years) than blacks (age mean is 36.85), and younger than the general population (age mean is 37.62). I also find that the Mexican average of completed years of education (9.88 years) is lower than the mean for blacks (12.47) and the mean of the general population (12.91). Mexicans also have a higher high school drop out rate than whites (De Freitas, 1991). Thus, what the estimates in Tables 3.1 and 3.3 are showing is that being Mexican, when human capital and structural variables are included as controls, does not make any difference if one compares Mexicans with similar non-Mexican workers in terms of underemployment likelihood.

Table 3.4 shows that the coefficient for Mexicans is positive in models (1), (3), (4), (5). However, when human capital variables are included in model (2), the coefficient for Mexicans becomes negative, with an odds ratio of 0.87. Therefore, what really explains the underemployment situation for Mexicans seems to be human capital theory. This conclusion is consonant with former studies of Mexicans that look at wages as the dependent variable (Reimers, 1992; De Freitas, 1990; Borjas and Tienda, 1985).

Summarizing, Tables 3.1, 3.3, and 3.4 show that aside the effects of structural variables, the main inequalities are among blacks and non-blacks, and female and male workers, since it is for these groups that their corresponding odds ratios are really different than 1. On the other hand, Mexicans seem to be essentially affected by human capital deficiencies. They tend to be younger and lower educated than their counterparts. Such findings suggest the existence of different social processes affecting diverse ethnic groups. Underemployment in the case of whites and blacks seems to be affected by both structural and human capital variables, while Mexicans are essentially suffering from low educational opportunities and lack of work experience. However, as Table 3.5 indicates, female workers, independently of ethnic group, are more likely to be in lower underemployment categories rather than in higher ones, relatively to male workers, a result that was hypothesized in Table 1.1 by human capital and neostructuralism due to discrimination against women. The same result would be expected according to efficiency wage theories based on the assumption that women have higher turnover than men (Katz, 1986).

Having discussed the differences in underemployment across ethnic and gender groups, it remains to analyze the effect of union membership on underemployment. This is the task in the next section.

The Effect of Unionization on Underemployment

Independently of the set of controls used in the ordinal model, the coefficient of the union membership dummy is always negative and significant in Tables 3.1, 3.3, 3.4, and 3.5. This means that being a union member makes workers more likely to be in higher underemployment categories rather than in lower ones vis-a-vis non-unionized workers. Moreover, the odds ratio corresponding to unionization is mostly of the order of 0.32, which indicates that union membership strongly increases the likelihood of being in higher underemployment categories with respect to non-unionized workers.

The results obtained for union membership validate hypotheses established in Table 1.1 following different underemployment theories. First, according to human capital/neoclassical economic theory, unionized workers enjoy an oligopolistic control on labor supply. Second, following neostructuralist theory, unionization increases worker power to set internal labor markets, therefore decreasing their vulnerability to underemployment. On the other hand, unionized jobs are linked to the core and state sectors (O'Connor, 1973), which gives workers further protection against underemployment.

In order to illustrate the interaction of gender, ethnicity, and unionization as determinants of underemployment, Table 3.7 shows the probabilities for different underemployment types corresponding to the ordinal model estimated in Table 3.6, which includes controls for human capital variables, ethnicity (black and Mexican), gender, and union membership.

The probabilities in Table 3.7 indicate that independently of being unionized or not, male workers have higher probabilities of being in full-time highly paid jobs than females across ethnic groups. Similarly, comparing men and women of the same ethnicity, female workers have greater or equal probabilities than men of being in every underemployment category. And comparing unionized with non-unionized workers, the latter have greater or equal probabilities of being in each category of underemployment vis-a-vis the former.

In sum, as the analysis of the probabilities in Table 3.7 indicates, the most disadvantaged among all groups tends to be the one formed by non-unionized black female workers. And among men, non-unionized black workers are the ones more vulnerable to underemployment.

CONCLUSION

Most results shown in Tables 3.1 to 3.7 are compatible with the expected results hypothesized in the summary Table 1.1. According to human capital theory, experience (age) and education decrease the chances of being underemployed. However, since the coefficient for age squared is positive, the advantage given by experience decreases in time, as human capital theory specifies. On the other hand, as neoclassical and human capital theory postulate, blacks and women are more vulnerable to underemployment than white men, as are nonunionized workers vis-a-vis the unionized ones. A distinct result is obtained for Mexicans, whose underemployment situation is very similar to that of the non-Mexican and non-black workers.

The former results can be reinterpreted along neo-structuralist lines as well. Worker underemployment decreases with age, education and union membership because worker power is higher in unionized settings, and workers have access to internal labor markets within unionized firms. Another factor could be that education acts as a credential or as an indicator of trainability (Thurow, 1975; Berg, 1970).

But an interpretation following efficiency wage theories is also consistent with most of the results shown above. The differences in underemployment across industrial sectors suggests that the mechanisms advanced by efficiency wage theories applied to underemployment could work: there might be differences in turnover, shirking, negative selection, unionization, or gift exchange norms acting throughout industries that produce differences in underemployment probabilities.

It is reasonable to consider that all the former mechanisms may add some contribution to the explanation of underemployment, as has been the conclusion in other studies that focus on wages (England, 1992; Krueger and Summers, 1988; Hodson, 1983) or unemployment (Schervish, 1983). However, what the ordinal model also shows is that there is no support for the deindustrialization hypothesis of Bluestone and Harrison (1980, 1988), and that the mechanism of underemployment works unequally across ethnic groups, since Mexicans are mainly affected by human capital deficiencies, in contrasts to blacks and whites, for whom structural variables are also significant to explain underemployment.

In the next chapter, an alternative model to the ordinal polytomous logistic regression is introduced. Then the hypotheses on Table 1.1 are tested again by using this model.

Table 3.1   Ordinal Logistic Regression Model with controls for
human capital and economic sectors, 1989.

Variable	Parameter Estimate	Odds Ratio
Intercept 1	-0.72*	0.49
Intercept 2	2.74**	15.51
Intercept 3	3.42**	30.65
Intercept 4	4.34**	76.88
Age	-0.20**	0.82
Age Squared	0.002**	1.00
Education	-0.11**	0.90
Black	0.26**	1.30
Mexican	-0.06	0.95
Female	0.60**	1.82
Union Member	-1.15**	0.32
Managers, Professionals, Executives, and Administrators	-1.33**	0.27
Technicians, Sellers, and Administrative Support	-0.77**	0.46
Service Occupations	-0.13*	0.88

Table 3.1   (Continued)

Variable	Parameter Estimate	Odds Ratio
Core	-0.43**	0.65
State	-1.11**	0.33

N = 12,769
-2 Log L = 16,335.58
Chi-Square for Covariates = 1728.908 (df = 12), p = 0.0001

  *p < 0.05
**p < 0.01

Note. The dependent variable is the cumulative logit of being in a lower underemployment category rather than in a higher. The data source is CPS 1990.

Table 3.2   Ordinal Logistic Regression with controls for Human
             Capital and Geographic Regions, 1989.

Variable	Parameter Estimate	Odds Ratio
Intercept 1	-0.03	0.97
Intercept 2	3.42**	30.47
Intercept 3	4.09**	59.59
Intercept 4	4.97**	144.65
Age	-0.21**	0.81
Age Squared	0.002**	1.00
Education	-0.17**	0.84
Midwest	0.21**	1.23
South	0.20**	1.22
West	0.16**	1.17

N= 12,769
-2 Log Likelihood= 16,915.92
Chi-Square for Covariates= 1148.57 (df= 6), p= .0001

*p < 0.05
**p < 0.01

Note. The dependent variable is the cumulative logit of being in a
lower underemployment category rather than in a higher. The data
source is CPS 1990.

Table 3.3   Ordinal Logistic Regression with controls for human capital, occupations, and industrial sectors, 1989.

Variable	Parameter Estimate	Odds Ratio
Intercept 1	-1.59**	0.20
Intercept 2	1.87**	6.50
Intercept 3	2.56**	12.91
Intercept 4	3.48**	32.63
Age	-0.19**	0.82
Age Squared	0.002**	1.00
Education	-0.11**	0.90
Black	0.29**	1.33
Mexican	-0.04	0.96
Female	0.69**	1.99
Union Membership	-1.13**	0.32
Managers, Professionals, and Administrators	-1.53**	0.22
Technicians and Administrative Support	-0.98**	0.38
Service Occupations	-0.37**	0.69

Table 3.3   (Continued)

Variable	Parameter Estimate	Odds Ratio
Agriculture, Forestry, and Fisheries	1.06**	2.88
Mining	0.66*	1.95
Construction	1.13**	3.98
Manufacture	0.22	1.25
Wholesale and Retail Trade	1.00**	2.73
Service Industry	0.96**	2.61
Transportation, Communications, and Public Utilities	0.09	1.09

N= 12,769
-2 Log Likelihood= 16,217.61, Chi-Square (df=17)= 1846.87;
p-value < 0.001
*   p < 0.05
** p < 0.01

Note. The dependent variable is the cumulative logit of being in a lower underemployment category rather than in a higher. The data source is CPS 1990.

Table 3.4   Estimation of several ordinal polytomous models that include different sets of covariates, 1989.

	Model				
Variable	*(1)*	*(2)*	*(3)*	*(4)*	*(5)*
Intercept 1	-6.49	0.06	-6.45**	-5.99**	-7.68**
	(0.14)	(0.21)	(0.14)	(0.14)	(0.17)
Intercept 2	-2.99**	3.61**	-2.95**	-2.47**	-4.17**
	(0.03)	(0.17)	(0.03)	(0.04)	(0.10)
Intercept 3	-2.39**	4.23**	-2.35**	-1.86**	-3.56**
	(0.03)	(0.17)	(0.03)	(0.04)	(0.10)
Intercept 4	-1.63**	5.06**	-1.59**	-1.10**	-2.79**
	(0.02)	(0.17)	(0.02)	(0.03)	(0.10)
Mexican	0.65**	-0.14*	0.65**	0.33**	0.61**
	(0.05)	(0.06)	(0.05)	(0.05)	(0.05)
Black	0.45**	0.36**	0.46**	0.26**	0.55**
	(0.05)	0.05)	(0.05)	(0.05)	(0.05)
Female	0.46**	0.53**	0.45**	0.75**	0.56**
	(0.03)	(0.03)	(0.03)	(0.03)	(0.03)
Age	--	-0.21**	--	--	--
		(0.01)			
Age Squared	--	0.002**	--	--	--
		(0.0001)			
Education	--	-0.18**	--	--	--
		(0.006)			
Union Membership	--	--	-1.33**	--	--
			(0.13)		

Table 3.4 (Continued)

			Model		
Variable	*(1)*	*(2)*	*(3)*	*(4)*	*(5)*
Managers, Professionals, Executives, and Administrators	--	--	--	-1.78** (0.56)	--
Technicians, Sellers, and Administrative Support	--	--	--	-0.94**	--
Service Occupations	--	--	--	-0.18** (0.04)	--
Agriculture, Forestry, and Fisheries	--	--	--	--	2.01** (0.12)
Mining	--	--	--	--	0.91** (0.23)
Construction	--	--	--	--	1.77** (0.11)
Manufacture	--	--	--	--	0.88** (0.11)
Transportation, Communications, and Other Public Utilities	--	--	--	--	0.48** (0.12)

Table 3.4 (Continued)

			Model		
Variable	*(1)*	*(2)*	*(3)*	*(4)*	*(5)*
Wholesale and Retail Trade	--	--	--	--	1.30** (0.10)
Service Industries	--	--	--	--	1.04** (0.10)
-2 log Likelihood	38,262	35,917	38,097	36,727	37,642

N= 25,916

** means $p < .01$
 * means $p < .05$

Note. Underemployment is formed by: (1) discouraged workers; (2) unemployed workers; (3) involuntary part-time workers; and (5) full-time workers paid above the poverty threshold (reference category). The dependent variable is the cumulative logit of being in a lower underemployment category rather than in a higher one. Standard deviations are in parentheses. The data source is CPS 1990.

Table 3.5   Ordinal Polytomous Models for Ethnic Groups, 1989.

Variables	Mexicans	Blacks	Others
Intercept 1	-1.4930 [0.1930]	-1.6475* [0.261]	-1.3423**
Intercept 2	2.1181** [8.315]	1.9925** [7.334]	2.2052** [9.073]
Intercept 3	2.8385** [17.090]	2.4788** [11.927]	2.8664** [17.574]
Intercept 4	3.8266** [45.906]	3.2245** [25.141]	3.7283** [41.606]
Age	-0.2398** [0.79]	-0.1265** [0.881]	-0.1939** [0.82]
Age Squared	0.0027** [1.00]	0.0011** [1.001]	0.0021** [1.00]
Education	-0.0803** [0.92]	-0.1452** [0.865]	-0.1223** [0.885]
Female	0.8126** [2.25]	0.6255** [1.869]	0.7475** [2.11]
Union Member	-1.0342* [0.35]	-1.5735** [0.207]	-1.1002** [0.33]
Managers, Professionals, Executives, and Administrators	-1.0436** [0.35]	-1.7433** [0.175]	-1.4404** [0.237]

Table 3.5 (Continued)

Variables	Mexicans	Blacks	Others
Technicians, Sellers, and Administrative Support	-0.8042** [0.48]	-1.0003** [0.368]	-0.9479** [0.388]
Service Occupations	-0.1328 [0.760]	-0.2739* [0.695]	-0.3635**
Agriculture, Fisheries, and Forestry	0.4709 [5.011]	1.6117** [2.243]	0.8077**
Mining	-1.0493	0.7946	0.4653
Construction	0.3451 [4.703]	1.5481** [2.765]	1.0169**
Manufacture	-0.4178	0.4899	0.1014
Transport, Communications, and Public Utilities	-0.3290	0.4258	0.0670
Wholesale and Retail Trade	0.1753 [3.752]	1.3223** [2.216]	0.7959**
Service Industries	0.1748 [2.364]	0.8605** [2.40]	0.8756**

Table 3.5 (Continued)

Variables	Mexicans	Blacks	Others
Midwest	0.6314 [1.216]	0.1364	0.1952**
South	0.8682	-0.0573	0.0361
West	0.7783 [1.198]	-0.1809	0.1807**
N	1770	2600	21550
-2 log Likelihood =	3155.227	4158.652	27344.089
Chi-Square =	280.259	494.138	3025.13
df	18	18	18
p -value <	0.001	0.001	0.001

Note. The dependent variable is the cumulative logit of being in a lower category rather than in a higher one. The odds ratios are shown in brackets. The data source is CPS 1990.

Table 3.6   Ordinal Polytomous Logistic Model with controls for human capital, ethnicity, gender, and unionization, 1989.

Maximum Likelihood Estimates

Variable	Estimate	St. Error	P-value	Odds Ratio
Intercept 1	0.0388	0.2105	0.8537	1.040
Intercept 2	3.5866**	0.1659	0.0001	36.110
Intercept 3	4.2123**	0.1660	0.000	67.514
Intercept 4	5.0388**	0.1670	0.0001	154.284
Age	-0.2093**	0.00861	0.0001	0.811
Age Squared	0.0022**	0.00011	0.0001	1.002
Education	-0.1813**	0.00580	0.0001	0.834
Black	0.3687**	0.482	0.0001	1.446
Mexican	-0.1437*	0.0603	0.0172	0.866
Female	0.162**	0.0320	0.0001	1.676
Union Membership	-1.1993**	0.1279	0.0001	0.301

N=25,916

Criterion	Intercept Only	Intercept and Covariates	Chi-Square for Covariates
-2 Log L	38,706.65	35,795.334	2911.316 with 7 DF

Inequality in the Workplace

P-value for the Chi-square = 0.0001
** means p < .01
 * means p < .05

Notes: The underemployment categories are: (1) discouraged workers; (2) unemployed workers; (3) involuntary part-time workers; (4) full-time low-wage workers; and (5) full-time workers paid above the poverty level (used as a reference category). The dependent variable is the cumulative logits of being in a lower category of underemployment versus being in a higher one. The data source is CPS 1990.

Table 3.7 Underemployment probabilities for male and female workers, 1989.

| | *Males* | | | | | |
| | *Unionized* | | | *Non-unionized* | | |
	Mexicans	*Blacks*	*Others*	*Mexicans*	*Blacks*	*Others*
Discouraged	0.00024	0.0004	0.0003	0.001	0.0013	0.001
Unemployed	0.01	0.014	0.01	0.03	0.05	0.03
Part-Time	0.01	0.012	0.01	0.02	0.03	0.03
Low-Wage	0.02	0.03	0.02	0.06	0.12	0.06
Full-Time	0.96	0.94	0.96	0.89	0.80	0.88
	Females					
	Unionized			*Non-unionized*		
	Mexicans	*Blacks*	*Others*	*Mexicans*	*Blacks*	*Others*
Discouraged	0.0004	0.001	0.0005	0.001	0.002	0.002
Unemployed	0.02	0.022	0.02	0.05	0.10	0.06
Part-Time	0.01	0.03	0.01	0.05	0.03	0.04
Low-Wage	0.03	0.05	0.04	0.10	0.12	0.10
Full-Time	0.94	0.90	0.93	0.80	0.75	0.80

N= 25,916

Notes. Workers selected are 35 years old, high school graduates. These probabilities are obtained from model (2), the ordinal polytomous logistic model. The covariates are: age, age squared, education, gender, Mexican ethnicity, black, and union membership. The data source is CPS 1990.

Chapter 4

A Multinomial Logit Model
of Underemployment

INTRODUCTION

The ordinal logistic regression model (2.1) and (2.2) estimated in Chapter 3 assumed that the dependent variable, underemployment, could be regarded as ordinal, according to the literature (Clogg, 1979; Clogg et al., 1986). This Chapter takes critically this assumption and offers an alternative view of underemployment. I argue that underemployment is a nominal variable. Therefore, the adequate model is not an ordinal polytomous logistic regression (Maddala, 1983), but a multinomial logit model (Judge et al., 1985). I also discuss the adequacy of this model versus possible alternative ones, namely, a multinomial probit model (Daganzo, 1979).

THE CRITIQUE OF THE ORDINALITY ASSUMPTION

My critique of the ordinal measurement level of underemployment has two dimensions: 1) Empirical, and 2) Theoretical. The empirical critique considers problematic the order of hardship in the labor market of the different categories of underemployment. Following Clogg et al. (1986), involuntary part-time workers would be facing a more difficult situation in the labor market than full-time low wage workers. However, Table 4.1 shows that there is a considerable number of involuntary part-time workers with higher wages than full-time low wage workers. Therefore, it is conceivable that some full-time low wage workers are facing a tougher situation in the labor market than some involuntary part-time workers. This suggests that the three dimensional hierarchical ordering of underemployment proposed by Clogg et al. (1986), with the purpose of depicting labor market hardship may not be adequate.

Table 4.1   Crosstabulation of Income Categories versus Involuntary Part-Time and Full-Time Low-Wage Workers, 1989.

| | *Income Categories* | | | | | | | |
	1	*2*	*3*	*4*	*5*	*6*	*7*	*8*
Involuntary Part-Time Workers	589	97	318	89	72	30	8	6
Full-Time Low-Wage Workers	1938	609	0	0	0	0	0	0

Source: Current Population Survey 1990, March Demographic File.

The theoretical critique sees the hierarchical order proposed by Clogg et al. (1986) as problematic. The priority of time of participation in the labor market over wage to determine levels of hardship in the labor market ignores the possible interaction between these two dimensions. In fact, such an interaction is an important part of the neoclassical model of the relation between leisure time and income (Hamermesh and Rees, 1988; Ehrenberg and Smith, 1991).

As Ehrenberg and Smith (1991) notice in their discussion of wait unemployment, some workers may decide not to accept a job until their reservation wage is satisfied, or until they can get a job in the primary sector of the economy. Thus, wait unemployment is an example of the interaction between wage and time of employment that violates the assumption that one dimension (time) should be considered before another one (wage).

Based upon this dual critique, the modeling of underemployment has to take into account its nominal, not ordinal measurement level.

A MULTINOMIAL LOGIT MODEL
OF UNDEREMPLOYMENT

Given that the ordinal nature of underemployment has been questioned, a second model is necessary without the assumption that the dependent variable is ordered. A viable model is the multinomial logit model (Agresti, 1990; Kmenta, 1986; Judge et al., 1985; Maddala, 1983) given by the following equations:

$$P[\ Y_i{=}5\ I\ X_i;\ B1,...,B5\ ]= 1/$$
$$[1{+}\exp(X_i'B1){+}...{+}\exp(X_i'B5)],$$
$$P[\ Y_i{=}j\ I\ X_i;\ B1,...,B5\ ] = \exp(X_i'Bj)\ /$$
$$[1{+}\exp(X_i'B1){+}...{+}\exp(X_i'B5)], j= 1,2,3,4, \tag{4.1}$$

Model (4.1) assumes that the probability that the ith worker is in the jth underemployment category is given by a logit function. Such probability depends on the jth underemployment category, since it is a function of the Bjs, and also depends on the vector X_i, formed by the independent variables. It is relevant to remark that this is an important difference with respect to models (2.1) and (2.2), in which the probability of a worker being in a certain underemployment category did not depend on different parameters B associated to those categories, i.e., B was constant across categories. In order to interpret the parameters estimated in (4.1), it is convenient to express this model in the following way:

$$\log\{P[\ Y_i{=}j\ I\ X_i;\ B1,..., B5\ ]/P[\ Y_i{=}5\ I\ X_i;\ B1,..., B5]\} = X_i'Bj, \tag{4.2}$$

Model (4.2) expresses the log-odds that the ith worker is in the jth category instead of in the fifth category. The fifth category, as was indicated above, corresponds to well-paid full-time workers. Thus, model (4.2) compares the likelihood of workers being underemployed versus not being underemployed, according to their individual and structural characteristics, given by the vector of independent variables X_i, which is the same as in model (2.2).

The estimation of model (4.2) would solve the problems related with the modeling of underemployment, but a look at one of the assumptions of model (4.2) may bring more problems ahead. Model

(4.2) assumes that the odds of being in a certain underemployment category versus not being underemployed do not depend upon any other category of underemployment. This assumption is called "the independence of irrelevant alternatives" (Judge et al., 1985; Hausman and McFadden, 1984; McFadden, 1974). If model (4.2) does not satisfy this assumption, it is inadequate to model underemployment. However, as Agresti (1990; p. 316) points out, the "application of the model should be limited to situations where the alternatives can plausibly be assumed to be distinct and weighed independently in the eyes of each decision-maker." Or, following Judge et al. (1985; p. 771), when the alternatives are close substitutes, the conditional multinomial logit model may not produce reasonable results.

Given the way the underemployment categories have been constructed, they are disjoint alternatives for workers. Each underemployment category reflects a totally different situation for workers than any other one. Therefore, they are not substitutes. A worker may be unemployed and there is no way in which she or he would also be discouraged, involuntarily part-time, or full-time low wage employed. This means that the assumption of "irrelevant alternatives" is valid for underemployment and a multinomial logit model is adequate to model it.

THE ESTIMATION OF THE MULTINOMIAL LOGIT MODEL OF UNDEREMPLOYMENT

The estimates of the parameters and its corresponding standard deviations of the multinomial logit model (4.2) are shown in Table 4.2. In that table, each column represents the logits of the corresponding underemployment category with respect to the baseline category, which is full-time fairly paid workers. For example, if one looks at the second column, it would give the following logit:

Log $(P2/P5)=3.42$ -0.22(Age) $+0.002$(Age square) -0.09(Educ) $+0.61$(Black) $+0.07$(Mexican) $+0.33$(Female) -1.51(Prof)-1.07(Tech) -0.32(Serv. Occ.) -0.03(Core) -0.59(State),   (4.3)

Table 4.2   Multinomial Logit Model for Economic Sectors, 1989.

		Logit		
Variable	*(P1/P5)*	*(P2/P5)*	*(P3/P5)*	*(P4/P5)*
Intercept	2.28	3.42**	2.07**	4.55**
Age	-0.37**	-0.22**	-0.15*	-0.24**
Age Squared	0.004**	0.002**	0.001**	0.003**
Education	-0.11	-0.09**	-0.13**	-0.12**
Black	0.53	0.61**	0.09	-0.01
Mexican	0.09	0.07	-0.20	-0.05
Female	1.13*	0.33**	0.67**	0.85**
Union Member	--	--	-0.23	-1.19**
Managers, Professionals, Executives, and Administrators	--	-1.51**	-1.26**	-1.22**
Technicians, Sellers, and Administrative Support	-0.70	-1.07**	-0.67**	-0.67**
Service Occupations	0.43	-0.32**	0.09	-0.05
Core	-0.13	-0.03	-0.53**	-0.83**
State	--	-0.59*	-1.66**	-1.25**

Table 4.2 (Continued)

N= 12,769

-2 Log Likelihood= 16,054.402

Likelihood Ratio Chi-Square (23468)= 9521.91,
p-value > 0.9

* p < 0.05,   ** p < 0.01

Notes:

   P1= Probability of being a discouraged worker.
   P2= Probability of being an unemployed worker.
   P3= Probability of being an involuntary part-time worker.
   P4= Probability of being a low wage full-time worker.
   P5= Probability of being a high wage full-time worker.

The dependent variable is the logit indicated at the top of each column. The reference category is full-time workers paid above 1.25 times the individual poverty threshold. The data source is CPS 1990.

   Therefore, in example (4.3), a variable with a significant negative coefficient has the effect of making a worker less likely (s/he has smaller odds) to be in the second category (unemployed workers) than in the baseline category 5 (fairly paid full-time workers). Analogously, if a variable has a significant positive coefficient, then that worker is more likely (the odds are higher) to be unemployed than full-time fairly paid. If the coefficients are exponentiated, what results are the odds ratios for the corresponding variables. Thus, based upon the guidelines to interpret the parameters of the model as was discussed in the example above, the following results are obtained:
   Tables 4.2 and 4.3 estimate a multinomial logit model with human capital and structural variables. The examination of the coefficients corresponding to discouraged workers indicates that this underemployment category is not influenced by structural determinants. Table 4.2 shows that younger workers, with less experience and training, are more likely to be discouraged than older workers.

Similarly, Table 4.3 shows that age, age squared, education, and being female are the only significant variables that influence discouragement. Thus, together, Tables 4.2 and 4.3 imply that what affects discouraged workers is being female or/and a lack of human capital investments. Discouraged workers tend to be younger, less educated, and female than workers with fairly paid jobs.

Table 4.3   Multinomial Logit Model for Industrial Sectors, 1989.

		Logit		
Variable	*(P1/P5)*	*(P2/P5)*	*(P3/P5*	*(P4/P5)*
Intercept	2.38	2.88**	1.36**	3.92**
Age	-0.28**	-0.20**	-0.17**	-0.24**
Age Squared	0.003**	0.002**	0.002**	0.003**
Education	-0.21**	-0.10**	-0.14**	-0.13**
Black	0.44	0.65**	0.02	0.03
Mexican	-0.50	-0.15	-0.10	-0.10
Female	1.01**	0.57**	0.85**	0.95**
Union Member	--	--	-0.42*	-0.90**
Professionals, Managers, Executives, and Administrators	--	-1.55**	-1.62**	-1.32**
Technicians, Sellers, and Administrative Support	-0.75	-1.10**	-1.10**	-0.85**
Service Occupations	0.12	-0.42**	-0.30**	-0.24**
Agriculture, Forestry, and Fisheries	0.07	0.75**	1.16**	1.17**

Table 4.3   (Continued)

| | *Logit* | | | |
Variable	*(P1/P5)*	*(P2/P5)*	*(P3/P5*	*(P4/P5)*
Mining	--	0.74*	0.16	0.18
Construction	0.15	1.17**	1.73**	0.46**
Manufacture	-0.65	0.27	0.34	-0.02
Transport, Communications, and Public Utilities	-0.52	0.18	0.66*	-0.12
Wholesale and Retail Trades	-0.41	0.77**	1.44**	0.77**
Service	0.56	0.48**	1.63**	0.86**

N= 25916

-2 Log Likelihood= 34,192.65

Likelihood Ratio (47900)= 20545, p-value > 0.9

 * $p < 0.05$
** $p < 0.01$

　　P1= Probability of being a discouraged worker.
　　P2= Probability of being an unemployed worker.
　　P3= Probability of being an involuntary part-time worker.
　　P4= Probability of being a low wage full-time worker.
　　P5= Probability of being a high wage full-time worker.

Notes, Table 4.3 continued:

The dependent variable is the logit indicated at the top of each column. The reference category for underemployment is full-time workers paid above 1.25 times the individual poverty threshold for 1989. The data source is CPS 1990.

Human capital variables are also significant in the cases of the other underemployment categories. Lack of human capital investments makes workers more likely to be unemployed, involuntary part-time employed, or to have low wage full-time jobs than to be full-time high wage workers, as was expected from human capital theory.

Analogously, for underemployment forms other than discouragement, industrial sector is a significant determinant. Workers within the state and core sectors are less likely to be involuntary part-time employed, or low wage full-time employed with respect to periphery workers. Also, workers in the state sector are more sheltered against unemployment than periphery workers, while workers in the core suffer unemployment as much as workers in the periphery.

The estimated coefficients for occupation mean that managers and professionals, as well as technicians are less likely to suffer from underemployment than blue collar workers. However, calculating the odds ratio for the only significant coefficient for service occupations gives 0.73, approximately 1. Therefore, workers in service occupations are as likely as blue collar workers to be underemployed.

Overall, the results for structural variables in Table 4.2 indicates that neostructuralist theory is supported. Workers enjoy more power as well as internal labor markets in the core and state sectors of the economy than in the periphery (O'Connor, 1973), and some occupations allow workers to be more sheltered to disadvantages in the labor market, particularly underemployment (Schervish, 1983).

Table 4.3, on the other hand, shows that efficiency wage theories (Yellen, 1984) are partially supported. The likelihood of underemployment varies across industrial sectors for every underemployment type, except discouraged workers. In particular, workers in whole sales and retail, service industries, construction, and agriculture are consistently more likely to be unemployed, involuntarily part-time employed, or low wage full-time employed vis-a-vis workers in the state administration sector.

Table 4.4 shows the results for a multinomial logit model that includes geographic region. These estimates indicate that underemployment varies across geographic regions. Workers in the Midwest are more involuntarily part-time employed and more low wage full-time employed than workers in the Northeast, the reference category. On the other hand, workers in the South suffer more low wage full-time employment than in the Northeast. Finally, workers in the West are as equally underemployed as those in the Northeast. Given that the deindustrialization theory (Bluestone and Harrison, 1980, 1988) hypothesized that workers in the Midwest would be the most affected by underemployment, these results offer only a partial support for this theory, since the Midwest equals the Northeast in at least two underemployment likelihoods: discouragement and unemployment.

Table 4.4   Multinomial Logit Model for Geographic Regions, 1989.

	Logit			
Variable	*(P1/P5)*	*(P2/P5)*	*(P3/P5)*	*(P4/P5)*
Intercept	3.95*	4.17**	2.64**	5.14**
Age	-0.38**	-0.23**	-0.16**	-0.26**
Age Squared	0.004**	0.002**	0.002**	0.003**
Education	-0.21**	-0.18**	-0.19**	-0.17**
Midwest	0.15	0.12	0.32*	0.24*
South	0.08	-0.03	0.22	0.38**
West	0.03	0.12	0.23	0.16

N= 12,769

-2 Log Likelihood= 16,821.81

Likelihood Ratio Chi-Square (8444)= 5228.06,
p-value > 0.9
*   p < 0.05
** p < 0.01

Notes:

P1= Probability of being a discouraged worker.
P2= Probability of being an unemployed worker.
P3= Probability of being an involuntary part-time worker.
P4= Probability of being a low wage full-time worker.
P5= Probability of being a high wage full-time worker.

The dependent variable is the Logit indicated at the top of each column. The reference category is full-time workers paid above 1.25 times the individual poverty threshold. The data source is CPS 1990.

The Mexican ethnicity coefficients in Tables 4.2 and 4.3 evidence that, after controlling for human capital for every category of underemployment, Mexicans are as likely as their complement, mostly whites, of being underemployed rather than having high paid full-time jobs, since none of the Mexican coefficients are significant. In the case of blacks, model (4.2), according to Tables 4.2 and 4.3, certifies that black workers are more likely to be unemployed than to have good jobs vis-a-vis non-black workers. However, black workers are equally likely to be discouraged, involuntary part-time employed, or in low wage full-time jobs as non-black workers are.

In the case of gender groups, female workers are consistently more likely than male workers to be in every underemployment category rather than to have a good job. This can be observed in both Table 4.2 and 4.3.

From the results using the multinomial logit model (4.2), it appears that gender groups are more different in their comparative underemployment situation than ethnic groups, net of additive human capital and industrial sector effects. Thus, according to the hypotheses from Table 1.1, the mechanisms of taste, statistical, and error discrimination are acting differently across ethnic and gender groups. Mexican males do not seem to face discrimination, as blacks and women do. However, blacks are discriminated against when they are actively searching for jobs, i.e., when they are unemployed. Discrimination does not seem to affect black workers in any of the other categories of underemployment.

Women face discrimination more than males. In every kind of underemployment category, women are more likely to be present than men. Moreover, if one adds the effects of ethnicity and gender together, black women are the most disadvantaged workers, since they are the group more likely to be underemployed across every underemployment category.

In sum, as was predicted by neostructuralism, efficiency wage, and human capital/neoclassical theory, blacks and women are more likely to be underemployed than whites and male workers. Nevertheless, the predictions for the case of Mexicans are not fulfilled.

The hypotheses about the effect of union membership on underemployment are also supported. Due to lack of cases in some cells (discouraged and unemployed workers), Tables 4.2 and 4.3 only show estimates for involuntary part-time and for full-time low wage workers. Such coefficients indicate, following neoclassical economic theory or neostructuralism, that unionized workers hold oligopolistic power that allows them to have a better chance of having good jobs instead of being underemployed vis-a-vis non-unionized workers. Furthermore, these coefficients also support efficiency wage theories of underemployment. According to these theories, unionized workers are self-selected and therefore, they are less likely to be underemployed.

It would be interesting to compare how the two models, the ordinal logistic regression model, and the multinomial logit model differ in their findings. Such discussion is offered in chapter 6.

CONCLUSION

The three dimensional hierarchical order of the underemployment categories, based upon time, wage, and attachment to the labor market, that was developed by Clogg et al. (1986) presents both theoretical and empirical problems. Empirically, there are, as shown by Table 4.1, many involuntary part-time workers with higher earnings than the full-time low wage workers. Thus, it is highly possible that some full-time low wage workers are facing a tougher situation in the labor market than some involuntary part-time workers. And theoretically, the dimensions that Clogg et al. (1986) consider hierarchically ordered may be interrelated, as the case of wait unemployment indicates (Ehrenberg and Smith, 1991).

These criticisms indicate that the correct model for underemployment is not ordinal polytomous regression, but a multinomial logit or probit model. As it turns out, the most difficult assumption to be satisfied by the multinomial logit model is the hypothesis of "independence of irrelevant alternatives". Such a property is approximately satisfied by underemployment. Therefore, a multinomial logit model as (4.2) is an adequate way to model underemployment.

The estimates of model (4.2) show that most of the hypotheses summarized by Table 1.1 are satisfied. Investments in human capital decrease workers' chances of being underemployed. Moreover, workers in the core and state sectors of the economy are more sheltered against underemployment than periphery workers.

The results for occupations also show that blue collar and service workers are more likely to suffer underemployment than other occupations.

Interestingly, deindustrialization theory is partially supported by the multinomial logit model, and discouraged workers seem to be affected by lack of human capital investments, not by structural constraints.

Ethnic groups face a very different underemployment situation. Mexican workers are as likely as whites to be underemployed, while black workers are more likely to be unemployed vis-a-vis non-black workers. With respect to other underemployment categories, black workers are in a similar situation to non-blacks. Nevertheless, female workers face more underemployment in every category than male workers. Moreover, the most affected group by underemployment is black women.

Thus, the results for ethnic and gender groups indicate that diverse forms of discrimination, after controls for human capital, occupations, and industrial sector are included, may still be present against blacks and women. One such form of discrimination might be the existence of different career ladders or internal labor markets for diverse ethnic or gender groups (Doeringer and Piore, 1971).

Chapter 6 elaborates more on the contrast between the two ways of modeling underemployment, as well as the implications for the stratification of the American labor force.

Chapter 5

Underemployment and Migration:
Does Foreign Origin Matter?

INTRODUCTION

Proficiency in the use of the English language has been shown to be a relevant determinant of worker's outcomes. Mexicans with good English ability tend to receive higher earnings than their counterparts with fair or poor dominion of such language (Bean and Tienda, 1987; De Freitas, 1991). Thus, Mexican immigrant workers, less likely to be proficient in the use of English, are more likely to be underemployed than the U.S. born Mexican workers. Furthermore, the concentration of Mexican immigrants in the West may increase their underemployment likelihood, relative to whites, due to the deindustrialization process that this region has experienced in the late 1980s (Bluestone and Harrison, 1982, 1988).

In this chapter, I investigate the difference in underemployment likelihood between U.S. born and immigrant workers. Such a comparison is made for Mexican, African American, and white non-Latino workers. Since the CPS 1990 does not include information about origin or English proficiency, several multinomial logit models are estimated using a different data set.

DATA AND METHODS

A cross-sectional analysis is performed for the year 1987. The source of data for this study is the June Current Population Survey (Fertility, Birth Expectations and Immigration File) for the year 1988 (U.S. Department of Commerce, 1988). This CPS (1988) data set includes items dealing with the demographic characteristics of the population as well as information on current employment status, work experience, occupation, industry, and income sources and amounts. The data used in this study includes samples restricted to individuals between the ages of 16 and 64, who are part of the civilian population. Next I discuss the operationalization of the variables.

Operationalization of the Variables

The operationalization of underemployment, the dependent variable, is the same as in Chapter 2. Since a new set of independent variables is included--origin, marital status, experience, and residence area--the operationalization of the independent variables is as follows:

The variable age minus education minus five (age-education-5) is used as the indicator of workers' experience. The information of the respondent's age is reported by the CPS (1988). Education is operationalized as the number of completed years of education.

Mexican ethnicity is operationalized by one dummy variable; it takes the value one if the respondent identifies him/herself as Mexican-American, Chicano(a), Mexican or Mexicano(a), and zero otherwise. African American ethnicity is operationalized by one dummy variable; it is one if the respondent is African American, zero otherwise. Similarly, the gender of the respondent is operationalized as one if the worker is female, and zero if male.

Occupational categories are operationalized following the two-digit code classification system employed by the U.S. Census Bureau, and reported by the CPS for its respondents' current or last job (U.S. Department of Commerce, 1988). The occupational categories used in the analysis are: (1) executives, administrators, managers, and professionals; (2) technicians, sellers, and administrative support; (3) service; (4) precision production, craft, and repair; (5) farming, forestry, and fishing; and finally, (6) operators, fabricators, and laborers. Five dummy variables are used to operationalize these categories, taking the sixth category as the base group.

As in the case of the statistical analyses in previous chapters, the individuals in the sample without previous experience in the labor force amount to less than 0.4 percent of the sample size. Since this proportion is very small, no special dummy variable has been assigned for them regarding occupation or economic sector.

The operationalization of the efficiency wage industrial sectors (Krueger and Summers, 1988) is based on the two-digit code for industry that the CPS provides for each respondent's current or last job, based on the Census Industry Classification System (U.S. Department of Commerce, 1988). The industry categories used in this analysis are: (1) agriculture, forestry and fisheries; (2) mining; (3) construction; (4) transportation, communications, and other public utilities; (5) wholesale and retail trade; (6) finance, insurance, and real estate; (7) miscellaneous services, entertainment, and recreation; (8) medical and hospitals; (9) welfare, religious, and education; (10) public administration; and (11) manufacturing. Ten dummy variables are constructed to operationalize these categories, using manufacturing as the base sector for comparison.

Three dummy variables operationalize union membership, marital status, and central city residence. The first dummy takes the value one if the worker is a union member, zero otherwise; the second dummy is one when the worker is married, zero in any other case, a variable that could be interpreted as a proxy for commitment to the job; and finally, the third dummy is one if the worker resides within the central city, and zero otherwise.

In order to operationalize origin, a dummy variable takes the value one if the worker is foreign born, and zero otherwise. Since this data set does not contain information on workers' language proficiency, the origin dummy could be used as an estimate of language proficiency in the case of immigrants from non-English speaking countries.

The Model

Underemployed workers are grouped in two nominal categories: (1) discouraged or unemployed workers; and (2) involuntary part-time or low wage full-time workers. The first category considers workers underemployed by being deprived of jobs, while workers in the second category, although being employed, are underemployed due to insufficient wages or employment hours. Since some authors suggest analyzing discouraged and unemployed workers separately (Buss and Redburn, 1988), the small percentage of discouraged workers in this study's samples (Table 5.1), impedes the consideration of discouraged workers as a separate category from unemployment.

Table 5.1   Means, Standard Deviations and Percentages of the Variables in the Analysis. Current Population Survey (June, 1988).

	Non-Latino Whites	*African Americans*	*Mexicans*
		Ethnic Group	
N	19,969	2,372	803
		Percentages	
Married	55.52	36.17	53.18
Unionized	9.03	11.26	7.35
Female	53.71	56.37	44.71
Foreign Born	9.49	9.23	39.85
Central City Resident	17.82	51.01	36.61
Occupation			
Operators, Fabricators and Laborers	15.26	22.85	26.40
Managers, Professionals and Executives	20.69	9.99	7.35
Technicians	32.79	25.55	21.54
Service	17.73	29.26	22.67
Craft	10.23	8.26	11.83

Table 5.1   (Continued)

| | Ethnic Group | | |
	Non-Latino Whites	*African Americans*	*Mexicans*
Farm	3.14	3.25	9.84
Industry			
Agriculture, Forestry and Fisheries	2.64	2.32	7.60
Mining	0.74	0.25	0.62
Construction	6.36	5.56	10.09
Wholesales and Retail Trade	25.99	21.75	25.90
Public Administration	4.00	5.19	3.36
Welfare and Education	9.46	10.16	7.72
Medical and Hospitals	7.73	8.43	5.23
Service	15.59	18.38	18.06
Finance, Insurance and Real Estate	5.91	3.63	2.86
Manufacturing	15.20	15.85	15.19

Table 5.1   (Continued)

Ethnic Group

	Non-Latino Whites	African Americans	Mexicans

Underemployment and Non-Underemployment Category

	Non-Latino Whites	African Americans	Mexicans
Discouraged Workers	0.42	1.31	0.50
Unemployed	10.35	23.78	17.93
Involuntary Part-Time	11.97	16.53	21.17
Full-Time Low Wage	2.45	2.82	2.99
Voluntary Part-Time	29.10	16.78	16.78
Full-Time High Wage	45.71	38.79	40.85

Means and Standard Deviations

	Non-Latino Whites	African Americans	Mexicans
Education	12.83 (2.47)	11.93 (2.46)	10.09 (3.51)
Age	34.81 (13.07)	33.56 (12.06)	32.42 (12.12)
Experience	15.98 (13.06)	15.63 (12.48)	16.32 (13.33)

A multinomial logit model (Agresti, 1990; Maddala, 1983) is estimated, using a third category of non-underemployed workers as the reference group, which is formed by voluntary part-time or high wage full-time workers. The following equations describe the model:

$$P[Wi1]= \exp(B1'Xi)/[1+\exp(B1'Xi+B2'Xi+B3'Xi)],$$
$$P[Wi2]= \exp(B2'Xi)/[1+\exp(B1'Xi+B2'Xi+B3'Xi)],$$
$$P[Wi3]= 1/[1+\exp(B1'Xi+B2'Xi+B3'Xi)], \qquad (5.1)$$

In model (5.1), $P[Wij]$ $j=1,2,3$ represents the probability that the ith worker in the sample is in the jth underemployment category. Thus, $P[Wi1]$ is the probability that the ith worker in the sample is a discouraged or an unemployed worker; $P[Wi2]$ is the probability that the ith worker in the sample is an involuntary part-time or a full-time low wage worker; and $P[Wi3]$ is the probability that the ith worker in the sample is a voluntary part-time or a full-time high wage worker. These probabilities depend on the vector Xi, formed by the independent variables, and the parameter vectors Bj, specific to each category. Model (5.1) could also be expressed in the following way:

$$\log\{P[Wi1]/P[Wi3]\}= B1'Xi,$$
$$\log\{P[Wi2]/P[Wi3]\}= B2'Xi, \qquad (5.2)$$

Model (5.2) expresses the log-adds that the ith worker is in the first or second underemployment category, against being in the third category, formed by non-underemployed workers. Thus, model (5.2) compares the likelihood of workers being underemployed versus not being underemployed, according to their individual and structural characteristics, given by the vector Xi.

Four multinomial logit models are estimated using the maximum-likelihood estimation technique. The findings are discussed next.

FINDINGS

Table 5.1 shows that the underemployment levels for the three groups considered, Mexicans, African Americans, and non-Latino whites, exceed largely the levels of unemployment for such groups. Adding the four underemployment categories—discouraged workers, unemployment, involuntary part-time work, and full-time low wage workers—the percentage of underemployed workers becomes 25.19, 44.44, and 42.59, for non-Latino whites, African Americans, and Mexicans, respectively. This means that approximately one quarter of white workers, and two fifths of African Americans and Mexicans are underemployed in 1987.

Table 5.1 also shows that on average, Mexican workers are younger, less educated, but have more experience than workers from the other two groups. Furthermore, the occupational percentages indicate that white workers are more than twice as likely to be represented among the managers, professionals, and executives, while Mexican workers are still over-represented in farm related occupations, as well as in the construction industry. On the other hand, the percentage of foreign born Mexicans (39.85 percent), is more than three times higher than the percentage corresponding to the other two groups considered: whites (9.49 percent), and African Americans (9.23 percent). Also, a high percentage of Mexicans are married (53.18 percent) compared to the percentage of married African American workers (36.17 percent), but comparable to the percentage of married whites (55.52 percent). Finally, Mexicans are second to African Americans in central city residence levels—36.61 percent versus 51.01 percent, respectively—compared to a much lower white central city residence level (17.82 percent).

Table 5.2 shows the estimates of a multinomial logit model for individuals of all ethnic and gender groups considered. Controls for human capital, structural variables, geographic residence, marital and immigration status are included. These results show that on one hand, female workers are less likely than male workers to be discouraged or unemployed rather than being full-time high wage or voluntary part-time employed, but on the other hand, female workers are more likely than males to be full-time low wage or involuntary part-time workers rather than full-time high wage or voluntary part-time workers. Similarly, Table 5.2 shows that African Americans and Mexicans are more likely than white non-Latino workers to be underemployed. Both minority groups are more likely than whites to be discouraged or unemployed, as well as full-time low wage or involuntary part-time, rather than full-time high wage or voluntary part-time employed.

Table 5.2   Multinomial Logit Model for Underemployment.
                   All ethnic and gender groups are considered.

Variable	Logit	
	ln(P1/P3)	*ln(P2/P3)*
Intercept	0.06	-.27**
	(0.13)	(0.13)
Education	-0.08**	-0.08**
	(0.01)	(0.01)
Experience	0.04**	-0.01
	(0.01)	(0.01)
Experience Squared	-0.001**	-0.00
	(0.0001	(0.0001)
Union Member	a	-1.62**
		(0.13)
Foreign Born	-0.22**	-0.16**
	(0.08)	(0.07)
Female	-0.08*	0.24**
	(0.05)	(0.05)
African American	0.91**	0.42**
	(0.06)	(0.06)
Mexican	0.49**	0.41**
	(0.11)	(0.10)
Occupations		
Managers, Professionals	-0.80**	-1.11**
	(0.08)	(0.09)

Table 5.2   (Continued)

Variable	Logit	
	ln(P1/P3)	*ln(P2/P3)*
Technicians	-0.56**	-0.66**
	(0.07)	(0.07)
Service	-0.22**	-0.01
	(0.07)	(0.07)
Crafts	-0.36**	-0.42**
	(0.08)	(0.08)
Farm	-0.03	0.48**
	(0.18)	(0.15)
Industries		
Agriculture, Forestry,		
and Fisheries	-0.59**	0.46**
	(0.20)	(0.17)
Mining	0.41**	0.26
	(0.21)	(0.30)
Construction	0.35**	1.15**
	(0.09)	(0.10)
Transportation		
and Utilities	-0.25**	0.29**
	(0.10)	(0.11)
Wholesale and		
Retail Trade	-0.39**	0.68**
	(0.07)	(0.08)
Finance, Insurance,	-0.67**	0.04
and Real Estate	(0.12)	(0.12)
Service Industries	-0.28**	0.81**
	(0.08)	(0.08)

Table 5.2   (Continued)

Variable	*Logit*	
	ln(P1/P3)	*ln(P2/P3)*
Medical and Hospitals	-0.67**	0.03
	(0.11)	(0.11)
Welfare and Education	-0.37**	0.48**
	(0.10)	(0.10)
Public Administration	-0.52**	-0.30*
	(0.13)	(0.16)
Married	-0.60**	-0.52**
	(0.05)	(0.05)
Central City Resident	0.19**	-0.03
	(0.05)	(0.05)

N=24,507
-2 Log Likelihood=33,954.64

Likelihood Ratio (34,427)=25,054.55,
p-value > 0.9

* $p < 0.10$; ** $p < 0.05$

Notes: a The number of discouraged or unemployed unionized workers in the sample is very small, therefore, no estimate has been calculated.

P1= Probability of being a discouraged or an unemployed worker.
P2= Probability of being an involuntary part-time or a full-time low wage worker.
P3= Probability of being a voluntary part-time or a full-time high wage worker.

Notes, contd: The dependent variable is the logit indicated at the top of each column. The reference category is the set of full-time workers paid above 1.25 times the individual poverty threshold plus the voluntary part-time workers. Standard Deviations are in parentheses. The data source is the CPS, June (1988).

The results shown by Table 5.2 indicate that human capital expectations are not fully supported. Education increases the likelihood of not being underemployed, but experience increases the chances that workers are more likely to be discouraged or unemployed than full-time high wage or voluntary part-time employed. Also, experience does not change the probability of being underemployed due to full-time low wage or involuntary part-time work, vis-a-vis voluntary part-time or full-time high wage employment. These results for experience contradict the expectations based on human capital theory. However, if being married is considered a proxy for job commitment, an individual characteristic of quality workers, Table 5.2 shows that married workers are less likely to be underemployed than non-married ones, a result that human capital theory anticipates (Smith, 1990).

As predicted by the monopoly and the voice of grievances arguments, union membership decreases the likelihood of being underemployed. Unionized workers are less likely to be full-time low wage or involuntary part-time employed, rather than being voluntary part-time workers or full-time high wage employees.

Differences in underemployment predicted by specialized human capital investments in occupations are confirmed by Table 5.2 results. Managers and professionals, technicians, and craft workers are less likely than operators, fabricators and laborers, to be in any of the underemployment categories rather than in the non-underemployment one. Alternatively, workers in farm occupations are more likely than operators, fabricators and laborers to be in full-time low wage or involuntary part-time jobs, instead of being non-underemployed. However, the chances of farm occupied workers are the same as those of the workers in the reference category of being discouraged or unemployed.

Workers in service occupations are less likely than laborers, fabricators and operators to be discouraged or unemployed, but equally likely to be in low wage full-time or involuntary part-time jobs than in the reference category of workers.

The results shown in Table 5.2 indicate that underemployment is unevenly distributed across industries. First, workers in the public administration sector are less likely to be in any of the underemployment categories, relative to workers in manufacturing. Second, workers in finance, insurance, and real estate, as well as workers in the medical and hospital industry, are less likely to be discouraged or unemployed than manufacturing workers; however, workers in the former sectors are as likely as those workers in the latter one to be in full-time low wage or involuntary part-time jobs.

The next group of industries includes: agriculture, forestry, fisheries, transportation, utilities, wholesale, retail trade, service, welfare and education. Workers in this group of industries are less likely than manufacturing workers to be discouraged or unemployed, but they are also more likely than manufacturing workers to be full-time low wage employed or in involuntary part-time jobs. Finally, in the group of industries formed by mining and construction, workers are more likely than manufacturing workers to be discouraged or unemployed; however, mining workers are equally likely, but construction workers more likely than manufacturing workers, to be underemployed due to full-time low wage or involuntary part-time employment.

Therefore, two broader industry groups can be distinguished. One is formed by public administration, finance, insurance, real estate, medical, hospitals, and manufacturing. In this group, workers are less or equally underemployed, but not more underemployed, than workers in manufacturing. The other group of industries is formed by the remaining industries shown in Table 5.2. Workers in such latter group of industries are more likely to be underemployed than manufacturing workers in at least one underemployment category.

Table 5.2 also shows that overall, foreign born workers are less likely to be underemployed than American born workers. Place of residence matters as well, since central city workers are more likely than suburban or rural workers to be discouraged or unemployed, but as likely as their counterparts to be employed in full-time low wage or involuntary part-time jobs, rather than having voluntary part-time or full-time high wage jobs.

Tables 5.3, 5.4, and 5.5 show the estimates of multinomial logit models for non-Latino whites, African Americans, and Mexicans, respectively. These models control for human capital including occupation, commitment to work—proxied by marital status—and residence within the central city. Controls for structural variables, such as union membership and industrial sector are also considered.

Table 5.3   Multinomial Logit Model for White, Non-Latino
                 Underemployment.

Variable	*Logit*	
	ln(P1/P3)	*ln(P2/P3)*
Intercept	-0.17**	-0.45**
	(0.16)	(0.15)
Education	-0.07**	-0.08**
	(0.01)	(0.01)
Experience	0.05**	-0.01**
	(0.01)	(0.01)
Experience Squared	-0.001**	0.00
	(0.0002)	(0.0001)
Union Membership	a	-1.60**
		(0.15)
Foreign Born	-0.35**	-0.39**
	(0.11)	(0.10)
Female	-0.11**	0.27**
	(0.06)	(0.05)
Married	-0.68**	-0.56**
	(0.06)	(0.05)
Central City Resident	0.17**	-0.02
	(0.06)	(0.06)
Occupations		
Managers, Professionals	-0.82**	-1.08**
	(0.10)	(0.10)

Table 5.3   (Continued)

Variable	Logit	
	ln(P1/P3)	*ln(P2/P3)*
Technicians	-0.61**	-0.64**
	(0.09)	(0.08)
Services	-0.22**	-0.01
	(0.09)	(0.08)
Crafts	-0.39**	-0.42**
	(0.09)	(0.09)
Farm	-0.18	0.54
	(0.22)	(0.17)
Industries		
Agriculture, Forestry, and Fisheries	-0.56**	0.37**
	(0.24)	(0.19)
Mining	0.48**	0.28
	(0.22)	(0.32)
Construction	0.37**	1.15**
	(0.10)	(0.11)
Transportation and Utilities	-0.15	0.33**
	(0.12)	(0.13)
Wholesale and Retail Trade	-0.37**	0.68**
	(0.08)	(0.09)
Finance, Insurance and Real Estate	-0.59**	0.08
	(0.13)	(0.14)

Table 5.3   (Continued)

Variable	Logit	
	ln(P1/P3)	ln(P2/P3)
Services	0.17	0.86**
	(0.09)	(0.09)
Medical and Hospitals	-0.69**	0.10
	(0.13)	(0.12)
Welfare, Religious and Education	-0.37**	0.56**
	(0.12)	(0.11)
Public Administration	-0.43**	-0.28
	(0.16)	(0.19)

N=19,969
-2 Log Likelihood=26,134.13

Likelihood Ratio Chi-Square (26,315)=18,013.84
p-value > 0.9

* p< 0.10,   ** p< 0.05

Notes: a The number of discouraged or unemployed unionized workers in the sample is very small, therefore, no estimate has been calculated.

P1= Probability of being a discouraged or an unemployed worker.
P2= Probability of being an involuntary part-time or a full-time low wage worker.
P3= Probability of being a voluntary part-time or a full-time high wage worker.

The dependent variable is the logit indicated at the top of each column. The reference category is the set of full-time workers paid above 1.25 times the individual poverty threshold plus the voluntary part-time workers. Standard Deviations are in parentheses. The data source is the Current Population Survey, June (1988).

Across the three ethnic groups studied, the effect of union membership and human capital investments decrease a worker's likelihood of being underemployed. However, an important exception is experience. In the case of non-Latino whites, experienced workers are more likely to be discouraged or unemployed than full-time high wage or voluntary part-time employed. In this same group's case, experienced workers are less likely to be in full-time low wage or involuntary part-time jobs than in the jobs comprised in the reference category of fair jobs.

Table 5.4   Multinomial Logit Model for African American
                 Underemployment.

Variable	*Logit*	
	ln(P1/P3)	*ln(P2/P3)*
Intercept	1.54**	0.65
	(0.37)	(0.40)
Education	-0.10**	-0.12**
	(0.03)	(0.03)
Experience	0.01	-0.01
	(0.02)	(0.02)
Experience Squared	-0.001**	-0.00
	(0.0004)	(0.0003)
Union Membership	a	-1.31**
		(0.28)
Foreign Born	-0.48**	-0.26
	(0.20)	(0.21)
Female	0.23*	0.24*
	(0.13)	(0.14)
Married	-0.66**	-0.34**
	(0.13)	(0.14)
Central City Resident	0.17	-0.18
	(0.11)	(0.12)
Occupations		
Managers, Professionals	-1.12**	-2.00**
	(0.28)	(0.43)

Table 5.4   (Continued)

Variable	Logit	
	ln(P1/P3)	*ln(P2/P3)*
Technicians	-0.54**	-0.66**
	(0.19)	(0.22)
Services	-0.25	0.10
	(0.20)	(0.21)
Crafts	-0.53**	-0.37
	(0.24)	(0.26)
Farm	0.73	1.00**
	(0.48)	(0.52)
Industries		
Agriculture, Forestry, and Fisheries	-0.95	0.27
	(0.58)	(0.60)
Mining	0.42	0.84
	(1.01)	(1.20)
Construction	0.72**	1.72**
	(0.28)	(0.30)
Transportation and Utilities	-0.33	0.31
	(0.25)	(0.30)
Whole Trade and Retail Sales	-0.35*	0.83**
	(0.20)	(0.24)
Finance, Real Estate and Insurance	-0.84**	-0.53
	(0.34)	(0.49)

Table 5.4   (Continued)

Variable	Logit	
	ln(P1/P3)	*ln(P2/P3)*
Services	-0.41	0.69**
	(0.21)	(0.25)
Medical and Hospitals	-0.76**	-0.31
	(0.27)	(0.33)
Welfare and Education	-0.60**	0.25
	(0.26)	(0.30)
Public Administration	-0.89**	-0.69
	(0.34)	(0.48)

N=2,372
-2 Log Likelihood=4,036.62

Likelihood Ratio Chi-Square (4,379)=3,775.79
p-value > 0.9
* p< 0.10, ** p< 0.05

Notes: a The number of unionized discouraged or unemployed workers in the sample is very small, therefore, no estimate has been obtained.

P1= Probability of being a discouraged or an unemployed worker.
P2= Probability of being an involuntary part-time or a full-time low wage worker.
P3= Probability of being a voluntary part-time or a full-time high wage worker.

The dependent variable is the logit indicated at the top of each column. The reference category is the set of full-time workers paid above 1.25 times the individual poverty threshold plus the voluntary part-time workers. Standard Deviations are in parentheses. The data source is the Current Population Survey, June (1988).

In the cases of African American and Mexican workers, experience does not make any difference to improve or worsen their chances of being underemployed. Therefore, these results for experience certainly contradict human capital theory.

Table 5.5   Multinomial   Logit   Model   for   Mexican
              Underemployment.

Variable	Logit	
	ln(P1/P3)	*ln(P2/P3)*
Intercept	0.41	-0.25
	(0.59)	(0.56)
Education	-0.07	-0.09**
	(0.04)	(0.04)
Experience	0.01	0.03
	(0.03)	(0.03)
Experience Squared	-0.00	-0.001*
	(0.0006)	(0.0005)
Union Membership	a	-1.53**
		(0.55)
Foreign Born	-0.57**	0.08
	(0.24)	(0.21)
Female	0.22	0.42*
	(0.24)	(0.22)
Married	-0.45*	-0.46**
	(0.24)	(0.22)
Central City Resident	-0.01	-0.19
	(0.21)	(0.20)
Occupations		
Managers, Professionals	-0.46	-0.91*
	(0.47)	(0.49)

Table 5.5   (Continued)

Variable	Logit	
	ln(P1/P3)	*ln(P2/P3)*
Technicians	-0.92**	-1.14**
	(0.37)	(0.36)
Services	-0.49	-0.13
	(0.35)	0.31)
Crafts	-0.01	-0.06
	(0.35)	(0.34)
Farm	-0.16	0.08
	(0.69)	(0.55)
Industries		
Agriculture, Forestry, and Fisheries	0.17	0.98
	(0.77)	(0.66)
Mining	0.27	0.84
	(1.26)	(1.24)
Construction	0.38	0.98**
	(0.39)	(0.42)
Transportation and Utilities	-1.05	0.31
	(0.80)	(0.64)
Wholesale and Retail Trade	0.14	1.11**
	(0.35)	(0.37)

Table 5.5   (Continued)

Variable	Logit	
	$ln(P1/P3)$	$ln(P2/P3)$
Finance, Real Estate and Insurance	-1.67 (1.08)	-0.69 (1.09)
Services	-0.66* (0.39)	0.83** (0.38)
Medical and Hospitals	0.28 (0.51)	0.70 (0.54)
Welfare and Education	-0.18 (0.50)	0.56 (0.51)
Public Administration	-1.78 (1.10)	0.07 (0.74)

N=803
-2 Log Likelihood=1,409.71

Likelihood Ratio Chi-Square (1,525)=1,376.44,
p-value > 0.9

* p< 0.10, ** p< 0.05

Notes: a The number of unionized discouraged or unemployed workers in the sample is very small, therefore, no estimate has been obtained.

P1= Probability of being a discouraged or an unemployed worker.
P2= Probability of being an involuntary part-time or a full-time low wage worker.
P3= Probability of being a voluntary part-time or a full-time high wage worker.

The dependent variable is the logit indicated at the top of each column. The reference category is the set of full-time workers paid above 1.25 times the individual poverty threshold plus the voluntary part-time workers. Standard Deviations are in parentheses. The data source is the Current Population Survey, June (1988).

The segmentation of human capital investments across occupations is also evident across the three ethnic groups considered. Workers in managerial, professional, or technical occupations, regardless of ethnicity, are less likely to be underemployed than workers in the reference occupational category, formed by operators, fabricators, and laborers. Craft white workers are also less likely to be underemployed vis-a-vis the baseline workers, but this is not true for minorities.

Craft Mexican workers are as likely as the reference group, Mexican operators, to be in either underemployment category. Craft African American workers are less likely to be discouraged or unemployed, but equally likely to be in low wage full-time jobs or to be involuntary part-time employed, rather than fairly employed.

In the case of workers in service occupations, whites are doing better than Mexicans and African Americans relative to operators. Whites are less likely to be underemployed as operators with respect to the first underemployment category, although equally underemployed with respect to the second one, while the latter two minority groups are both as likely to be underemployed as operators, independently of the underemployment category being considered.

Mexican and white workers in farm occupations are as likely as operators to be in either underemployment category. However, African American workers in farm occupations are more likely to be in low wage or involuntary part-time jobs than African American operators, but equally likely than the latter ones to be discouraged or unemployed.

Table 5.3 shows that in the case of industrial sectors, white workers are less likely to be discouraged or unemployed, but as likely to be involuntary part-time or low wage workers as their counterparts in the manufacturing sector if they are in finance, insurance, real estate, medical, hospitals, or public administration. White workers in the remaining industrial sectors are more likely to be underemployed than manufacturing workers in at least one underemployment category. Hence, the efficiency wage and employment industrial sector for white workers, as well as the non-efficiency wage and employment sector, coincide with the efficiency and non-efficiency sectors for all workers shown in Table 5.2.

As can be observed in Table 5.4, African American workers are less likely than manufacturing workers to be discouraged or unemployed, but equally likely to be involuntary part-time or low wage employed, in the same sectors pointed above as the efficiency wage and employment sectors for white workers as well as in welfare and education. However, in contrast to whites, African American workers are as likely to be underemployed as manufacturing workers in agriculture, forestry, fisheries, mining, transportation and utilities.

Mexican workers, as shown in Table 5.5, have a less well defined efficiency wage and employment sector than both whites and African Americans. Aside from construction, wholesale, retail trade, and services, where Mexican workers tend to be more underemployed than their counterparts in manufacturing within the second underemployment category, workers in the remaining industrial sectors are equally likely to be underemployed with respect to manufacturing workers.

Hence, the results from Tables 5.1 to 5.5 indicate that the efficiency wage and employment sector, observed in Table 5.1 for all workers, appears to shelter Mexicans and African Americans less than whites. This is so because minority workers in the efficiency wage industries are as likely to be underemployed as minority workers placed in non-efficiency wage industries. Therefore, such a situation suggests the possibility that employers in efficiency wage industries may discriminate against minority workers.

There are more similarities between Mexicans and African Americans. First, in contrast to non-Latino whites, for whom foreign origin decreases their underemployment likelihood, foreign born Mexicans and African Americans are as likely as their American born counterparts to be involuntary part-time or low wage employed. However, foreign born Mexicans and African Americans are less likely to be discouraged or unemployed than those American born. Second, central city residence, compared to residence in suburban or rural areas, does not change the underemployment likelihood of Mexicans or African Americans. In contrast, central city white residents are more likely to be discouraged or unemployed, although their likelihood with respect to the second underemployment category is not affected by residence.

In the case of Mexicans, the coefficient of national origin—a proxy for language skills—may seem to indicate that language proficiency, net of human capital and structural variables, is not relevant to improve the underemployment condition of Mexican Americans with respect to their counterparts born in Mexico.

Finally, African American, Mexican and white females are more likely than their male counterparts to be underemployed due to involuntary part-time or low wage full-time jobs. However, a female's underemployment situation differs with respect to the other underemployment category. While Mexican and African American females are as likely or more likely than their respective Mexican and African American male counterparts to be discouraged or unemployed, white female workers are less likely to share such problems with white male workers.

SUMMARY AND CONCLUSIONS

Using Current Population Survey (1988) data (U.S. Department of Commerce, 1988), which includes information on immigration status and labor market situation of workers, my results show that, after controlling for human capital, industries, union membership, geographic residence, and national origin, Mexican and African American workers remain more likely to be underemployed with respect to white workers. Such an underemployment gap might be caused by unmeasured human capital, such as worker's ability, but it is also possible that taste and statistical discrimination are a part of this process. White women, on the other hand, are less likely than white men to be discouraged or unemployed, but more likely to hold involuntary part-time jobs or full-time low wage employment. However, Mexican women are equally, and African American women are more, discouraged or unemployed than their male counterparts, although both groups are more likely to be in the second underemployment category—involuntary part-time or low wage full-time employed—with respect to Mexican and African American males, respectively.

Contrary to previous research that finds human capital variables as the sole determinants of Latino wages (Abowd and Killingsworth, 1985), and in contrast to some results in Chapter 3 (Table 3.5)—based on CPS (1990) data—which show no significant industrial determinants of Mexican underemployment, both human capital and structural variables are significant underemployment determinants for Mexicans, African Americans, and whites, when CPS (1988) is utilized. Hence the significance of economic sectors, as underemployment determinants for the case of Mexican workers, appears to vary longitudinally.

Mexicans have the same underemployment likelihood across the sector formed by manufacturing, financing, insurance, real estate, medical, hospitals, and public administration—the efficiency wage sector for whites. The situation for African Americans is analogous to Mexican workers; they are also equally likely to be underemployed across such an efficiency wage sector. However, the Mexican and African American likelihood of being underemployed in the efficiency wage sector equals that of being underemployed in the agriculture, mining, and construction industries, strongly affected by the 1980s economic recession (Bluestone and Harrison, 1982, 1988), which, as in the case of agriculture, are known to provide disadvantageous working conditions to its workers.

Thus, given that whites appear more sheltered against underemployment in the efficiency wage sector than Mexican and African American workers, discrimination might be a factor involved in the underemployment likelihood difference across these three ethnic groups, as hypothesized by efficiency wage theories.

Furthermore, the findings for Mexicans show that, net of human capital and other structural variables, language proficiency is not relevant to explain underemployment. Foreign and American born Mexicans have the same likelihood of being involuntary part-time or low wage employed, and foreign born Mexicans are less likely to be discouraged or unemployed than their Mexican American counterparts, after controlling for relevant labor market characteristics.

Finally, this study also suggests the need to investigate if the effects of experience on underemployment likelihood, null in the cases of both minority groups considered (Tables 5.4 and 5.5), and positive for white workers, thereby increasing their likelihood of being discouraged or unemployed (Table 5.3), are due to particular circumstances during the year of the analysis (1987), or are part of a more extended trend.

Chapter 6

Conclusions

THE QUESTIONS AND THE THEORIES

This study has discussed the following questions:
1. How can we explain underemployment?
2. Which is the best way of modeling underemployment?
3. Are there differences in underemployment net of (but additive to) human capital, occupations, and industrial sectors, across gender and ethnic groups? And, what explains these differences?

I presented four theories which explain underemployment: human capital theory (Becker, 1964), neostructuralism (Averitt, 1968; Schervish, 1983; Hodson, 1983), deindustrialization theory (Bluestone and Harrison, 1980), and efficiency wage theories (Katz, 1986).

Human capital theory (Becker, 1964) maintains that investments in education, on-the-job training, and migration increase worker productivity, which in turn makes workers less vulnerable to become underemployed, i.e., discouraged, unemployed, involuntarily part-time or full-time low wage employed. The hypothesis obtained from this theory is that higher investments in education or training decrease the probability of being underemployed.

Neostructuralism (Schervish, 1983; Fligstein et al., 1983) looks at the environment where workers are employed and how these surroundings constrain their outcomes, like wages or underemployment. The type of firm, organization, occupation, class, or industrial sector where the worker is, determines the extent of the benefits or protection workers receive for their investments in human capital (Wright, 1979), and directly influences labor outcomes, particularly underemployment.

Several neostructuralist hypotheses are important for this study. First, workers in the periphery (Hodson, 1977; Beck, Horan, and Tolbert II, 1978) are more likely to be underemployed than workers in the core or the state sectors of the economy. And second, that blue collar and service occupations workers are more vulnerable to underemployment than workers in the executive, managerial, professional, or technical occupations.

Deindustrialization theory (Bluestone and Harrison, 1988, 1980) adds to neostructuralist theories a more dynamic view of the transformations of the U.S. economy. It maintains that during the last two decades, there has been a process of capital migration within and out of the United States, as well as a trend of lower industrial investment in the country. Consequently, deindustrialization has affected the American economy, particularly the Midwest, more than the other regions of the country. Therefore, underemployment has become unequally distributed across the country's geographic areas—workers in the Midwest being the most vulnerable.

The last group of explanations of underemployment comes from efficiency wage theories (Yellen, 1984; Katz, 1986). These theories originated as an intent by mainstream economists to explain differences in wages across industries. The general idea of efficiency wage theories is that wages influence worker effort, which in turn affects firm productivity. Thus, firm productivity may be increased by augmenting the wage. Since there are different firm production functions, there are different wages that maximize firm productivity.

I have extended efficiency wage theories to explain underemployment. The idea is that along with wages, worker effort may be increased (or decreased) by the type of job assigned, for example, part-time or full-time. Workers with full-time jobs may tend to be more productive than involuntary part-time workers, since having full-time jobs may increase the group labor norms (Akerlof, 1984; 1982). Workers may engage in gift exchange behavior where more effort corresponds to full-time, or even to extended part-time jobs. Workers with full-time jobs may also avoid shirking, turnover, negative selection, or may decide to avoid unionization. All these decisions may result in increased worker effort that corresponds to higher firm productivity, more in some industries than others (Katz, 1986).

I also extended efficiency wage theories formally to show that they can include human capital variables, as well as other structural determinants besides industries, such as occupations. Thus, through efficiency wage theories, one can integrate theoretically several different perspectives on underemployment. This is an alternative synthesis to the one done by neostructuralist authors (Fligstein et al., 1983). Furthermore, the relevance of efficiency wage theories for underemployment was tested in this study.

The test of the hypotheses presented above has not been straightforward. The methodological part became an important problem, since theoretical and methodological issues were closely linked to the alternative models used.

WHAT IS THERE IN A MODEL?
THE MODELING OF UNDEREMPLOYMENT

In order to test the hypotheses obtained in Chapter 1 and summarized in the previous section, it has been necessary to find an adequate model. Clogg et al. (1986) argue that underemployment is an ordinal categorical variable. The order is defined by a hierarchical tri-dimensional vector composed by: (1) the time a worker is employed; (2) the wage a worker receives; and (3) the attachment to the labor market, i.e., participation or non-participation in the labor market.

However, the modeling of underemployment is not so straightforward. The use of an ordinal logistic regression model rests on the assumption that the argument advanced by Clogg et al. (1986) really works. I advanced two critiques against the tri-dimensional ordering argument, one theoretical and another empirical: First, the time, wage, and attachment dimensions might not be hierarchical. The theory of leisure and employment, for example (Ehrenberg and Smith, 1991), argues for the interrelation between wages and time of employment, as in the case of wait unemployment, where some workers decide to wait unemployed until an adequate job that satisfies their reservation wage is found. Thus, the amount of the wage is determining the time of participation in the labor market, a clear violation of the hierarchical principle advanced by Clogg et al. (1986). This argument might also be compatible with efficiency wage theories. Workers may think that employers would rate them low if they accept a bad job, given that a highly productive worker would be highly selective (Katz, 1986).

Second, I found that there are many involuntary part-time workers with higher wages than full-time low wage workers. Therefore, it is

difficult to argue, as Clogg et al. (1986) do, that all involuntary part-
time workers would be facing more hardship than all full-time low
wage workers, especially if some involuntary part-time workers are
receiving substantially higher wages than full-time low wage workers.

These critiques mean that model (2.2) is not the adequate model for
underemployment. Instead, the appropriate model has to take into
account the nominal character of the dependent variable.

Two models could deal with the nominal character of
underemployment. One is the multinomial logit model, and the other is
the multinomial probit model (Judge et al., 1985; Daganzo, 1979). The
latter is more general than the former one because it can include cases
where the categories of the dependent variable are or are not
independent, but one advantage of the multinomial logit model is that
it has a nice interpretation in terms of logits. Also, the multinomial
logit model requires the assumption of "independence of irrelevant
alternatives", which means that the logit of the alternatives being
compared is functionally independent of the remaining alternatives.

I have argued in Chapter 4 that underemployment satisfies the
assumption of "irrelevant alternatives", since the underemployment
categories are not close substitutes for each other. This means that it is
not necessary to estimate a multinomial probit model of
underemployment.

Does it matter which model was used between the ordinal logistic
regression and the nominal multinomial logit? A look at the summary
Table 6.1 may suggest that the two models are essentially providing the
same results. This is not the case. The two models work in a totally
different way. On one hand, the ordinal model establishes a hierarchy
of underemployment categories. In such a case, every underemployment
category is compared to all the others. On the other hand, the nominal
multinomial logit model compares every underemployment category to
a reference category, i.e., high wage full-time workers. Thus, the results
of the first model have to be interpreted differently from the results of
the second model, since the nature of the comparisons is very different.
For example, an increase in age, under the ordinal model increases the
likelihood of being in a higher underemployment category, while under
the nominal model, an increase in age increases the likelihood of being
in the reference category (high wage full-time workers), rather than in
a particular underemployment category. Thus, in the first case all
categories are compared at once, while in the second, the comparison
is between two categories at a time.

The ordinal and the multinomial logit models have been estimated to compare the results obtained under both situations. The findings, as I summarize next, show that the distinction between the two models is important.

Table 6.1 Summary of findings.

Human Capital			
Support		*Challenge*	
Model		*Model*	
Ordinal	M-L	Ordinal	M-L
Age	Age	Discrimination	Discrimination
Education	Education	Structural Effects	Structural Effects
Efficiency Wage and Structuralism			
Support		*Challenge*	
Model		*Model*	
Ordinal	M-L	Ordinal	M-L
Industrial Sectors	Industrial Sectors	Mexicans (1990)	Mexicans (1990)
Occupations	Occupations	Discouraged Workers	Discouraged Workers
	Experience (1988)		

Table 6.1 (Continued)

		Deindustrialization		
Support			Challenge	
Model			Model	
Ordinal	M-L	Ordinal		M-L
Whites	Involuntary Part-time and low-wage workers in the Midwest and the South			Other Regions (besides the Midwest) present

Northeast
workers most
sheltered

Notes. The findings are arranged according to the support and challenge
of the main theories utilized in this study. The data sources were CPS
1990, and CPS 1988.

HUMAN CAPITAL THEORY:
IS IT SUPPORTED?

The explanation of underemployment, as well as the analysis of the
underemployment differences across ethnic and gender groups has been
explained by several competing theories. Table 6.1 shows a summary
of the findings of this study. They are classified by theory and models.

Human capital theory (Becker, 1964) is supported by both the
ordinal and the multinomial logit models, based on the analysis of CPS
(1990) data; however, human capital's expectations are questioned by
the analysis based on CPS (1988) data.

In the analysis of CPS (1990) data, age is used as a proxy for
experience, although it is a better approximation for male than for
female workers (Hodson and England, 1986). These two variables,

along with age squared, support, in both models, the hypothesis that investments in human capital decrease the likelihood of worker underemployment. Higher educational attainments and increased amounts of experience in the labor market make workers more likely to be in higher categories of underemployment rather than in lower ones, vis-a-vis workers with less amounts of experience or education, according to the ordinal logistic regression model. In the case of the multinomial logit model, more years of education and experience decrease the odds of being in any of the underemployment categories versus being a high wage full-time worker. In both models, the age square coefficient is always positive indicating that the advantage of investing in human capital decreases when workers become older. This is due, as human capital theory explains, to skill depreciation in time and to a decrease in workers investments in human capital, since their expected returns diminish with age.

The analysis of CPS (1988) shows, on the other hand, that the effect of experience (defined as age minus education minus five), increasing the likelihood of white workers to be discouraged or unemployed, does not correspond to the expected effect of experience hypothesized by human capital theory (Table 5.3). Furthermore, experience does not make the likelihood of underemployment any different for Mexican or African American workers (Tables 5.4 and 5.5), in contradiction to human capital theory as explained in Chapter 1.

Thus, the differences between the effects of human capital variables on worker underemployment, presented above in the cases of CPS (1990) and CPS (1988), allow me to hypothesize that the effect of human capital on the underemployment likelihood of workers, contrary to the static view of some neoclassical economists, may vary across the business cycle.

But the presence of significant structural effects in both models challenges human capital theory. Both industrial sectors and occupations have significant effects under the two models. This fact violates human capital expectations, since competition is supposed to eliminate differences across industrial sectors and occupations. Neoclassical economists argue that once workers realize that they are becoming more underemployed in some sectors of the economy, they will go to those sectors that offer them better employment perspectives, which in turn is going to cause underemployment to increase in such sectors, equalizing the underemployment likelihood across all of them.

The presence of structural effects on underemployment is questioned by neoclassical economists. Unmeasured human capital might be the reason these effects appear to be significant (Smith, 1990). Neoclassical economists argue that the proxies used to control for human capital are not very sensitive to variations across individuals. In the case of education, for example, it is assumed that all individuals are receiving the same kind of education, that is, that no controls are set for the educational quality. While it is true, orthodox economists would argue, that blacks and whites have approximately the same educational distribution, the quality of their education is very different. This would affect their underemployment likelihood, according to these economists.

Human capital is not well measured for another reason. Education and work experience do not catch the effect of ability. Some individuals are more talented than others (Smith, 1990). Thus, educational achievement and age effects would be underestimating and overestimating the effect of human capital on the underemployment chances of workers (Ehrenberg and Smith, 1991; Hamermesh and Rees, 1988).

And finally, orthodox economists argue that occupational effects could be reconciled with human capital theory. Occupations could be considered as indicators of skill level (Smith, 1990), or give workers the possibility of performing some restriction over the supply of labor (Becker, 1975; Friedman, 1962).

Industrial sector effects have been present in studies of wages across time, during long periods, in both time series and crossnational studies performed in different countries (Thaler, 1989; Katz, 1986; Dickens and Katz, 1987). Therefore, if the equilibrium mechanisms that neoclassical economists support were to be present, they had already had enough time to act. And they have not. Furthermore, Thaler (1989), and Dickens and Katz (1987) argue that orthodox economists have too much faith in the unmeasured human capital investments, because even if these variables are missing, they still are correlated with the proxies for human capital already used. Therefore, these variables are already catching most of the effects of ability and quality of education, for example.

The only structural variable admitted by neoclassical economists is unionization. Unions are understood as oligopolies by these economists (Ehrenberg and Smith, 1991). They have an oligopoly effect on labor by restricting its supply to the labor market (Freeman and Medoff, 1984). Unions are also seen as means of collective voice and institutional response that provide an alternative change mechanism (Freeman and Medoff, 1984). Thus, it is no surprise to neoclassical economists that unionized workers are less vulnerable to underemployment in comparison to non-unionized workers. And indeed, both models verified this hypothesis in Chapters 3, 4 and 5.

Neostructuralist authors agreed with the former interpretation of union membership effects on worker outcomes, although they call the oligopolistic effect a "power effect". However, for neostructuralists, there is another reason that unionization decreases underemployment. Unions support the creation of internal labor markets within the firm, which protects workers against underemployment. Thus, according to neostructuralists, internal labor markets are a product of labor power.

Neoclassical economists do not recognize internal labor markets as a product of worker power. Instead, they support the idea that this internal organization is due to efficiency considerations within the firm (Smith, 1990). This controversy remains unsolved due to the difficulties in gathering the adequate data to test the alternative mechanisms involved (Smith, 1990).

A second challenge to human capital theory is the existence of discrimination. After controlling for individual and structural variables, there still is a significant effect for black workers (Tables 3.1, 4.2 and 5.2). The likelihood of underemployment is higher for African Americans than for white workers under both models. Such an underemployment gap for African Americans is present across CPS (1990) and CPS (1988) data sets.

The evidence for women shows that female workers are more underemployed than men using CPS (1990) data. However, the analysis based on CPS (1988) data shows that women are less likely to be underemployed in some categories of underemployment, namely, involuntary part-time and low wage full-time work, while men are more likely than women to be discouraged or unemployed.

As in the case of women, Mexicans are more underemployed than white, non-Latino workers in 1987. However, in 1989 the likelihood of underemployment between Mexicans and whites is the same.

Thus, the case for the presence of labor market discrimination against African Americans is stronger than against Mexicans or women, whose situation may vary across the business cycle. Some neoclassical economists recognize the existence of discrimination as a residual effect on underemployment. Discrimination constitutes another obstacle to economic equilibrium. In consequence, neoclassical economists elaborate theories of discrimination based on the taste of the employers or the employees (Becker, 1971), and on statistical discrimination (Ehrenberg and Smith, 1991).

Taste discrimination occurs when either employers or employees have a preference for a certain group over another. In some cases, employers do not mind hiring workers from certain ethnic or gender groups, but their employees may pressure them to hire members of one group over another. And in some other cases, it is employers who avoid hiring females or minority workers.

Statistical discrimination is a case of the ecological fallacy. Employers may know or believe that one ethnic or gender group is more productive than another one. Then they infer that any individual from the more productive group is more productive than any individual from the less productive group. Thus, individuals are assigned the average productivity of their group without taking into account the within group variations. It is also possible that employers know there is error in their individual measurements, but because of information costs, it is cheaper to get some information from gender and ethnic characteristics, than to ignore them or to incur the expense of an improved individual measure.

Therefore, following taste or statistical theories of discrimination, neoclassical economists would interpret the significant coefficients for blacks, Mexicans and females, obtained by the ordinal or nominal models, as evidence of taste or statistical discrimination against black, Mexican and female workers.

The assumption of different productivity of workers belonging to different groups, net of other influences, such as human capital and structural variables, that some neoclassical economists have made, is questioned in the case of female and male workers by England (1992). There is no unquestionable evidence that male workers are more productive than women, independently of measured individual and structural characteristics. Similarly, Gordon (1972) questions the existence of differences in productivity between whites and minority workers. Thus, statistical discrimination may be in reality error discrimination (England, 1992). Employers believe, although erroneously, that one group is more productive than others, and they proceed in consequence, hiring workers that belong to the group they believe is the most productive one.

Taste discrimination is not free of problems. Neoclassical economists consider taste as exogenously determined in their model, therefore they do not worry about its explanation. But for sociologists this is a problem in itself. Why would employers or employees have a preference in favor or against some group or groups?

In the case of employees, a possible answer is that what really is going on in the labor market between groups of workers is antagonism, and that is what determines the group "taste". Such antagonism between two or more groups of workers may be due to a split labor market along ethnic or gender lines (Bonacich, 1972).

According to Bonacich (1972), the labor market may split because there are two or more groups of workers whose labor price differs for the same work. The wage is determined by the standard of living or economic resources of the workers, the level of information or ignorance of workers, and the political resources or level of organization of groups of workers.

The "taste" of white male workers against minorities is in reality antagonism against the weak group. As Bonacich (1972) explains, the more resourceful group is threatened by the weakness of the less resourceful group. The solution envisioned by the powerful group ranges from total exclusion of the weak group from the labor market, to the organization of a caste system, i.e., to weaken the weak group even further, until it is of no use to the employers because of lacking the useful work skills.

The "taste" of employers may have to adjust to political and economic pressures from organized labor, in order to favor the most powerful group, even if it is convenient for employers to organize a free market, since competition would lower the price of labor for all groups (Bonacich, 1972).

Alternatively, Reich (1981, 1971) argues that the capitalist class purposefully plays off one segment of the working class against the other. Therefore, the result of class antagonism is that the whole working class is weakened. In this way, workers become more vulnerable to low wages and underemployment.

Yet a third argument advanced by structuralist authors, is that discrimination exists beyond the firm's ports of entry (Doeringer and Piore, 1971). Indeed, discrimination can often be found within the firm. Minority workers, including women, could be placed in different internal labor markets within the same firm or corporation. Thus, although apparently all ethnic and gender groups are equally admitted into the firm, the reality is that the career ladders may be different across these groups. This may help to explain why even after controlling for human capital and structural variables, there still is an effect of gender and ethnicity in the estimates of the models.

In sum, of the two explanations of discrimination offered by neoclassical economics, statistical discrimination has not been unquestionably supported by empirical evidence, and "taste" discrimination presents the problem of avoiding the explanation of the origin of such preferences. In this respect, structuralist theories have done a better job. However, the importance of human capital variables as determinants of underemployment is unquestionable. Is that the case of structuralist theories of underemployment?

NEOSTRUCTURALISM AND EFFICIENCY WAGE THEORIES OF UNDEREMPLOYMENT: THE FINDINGS.

As Table 6.1 shows, the presence of structural variables in the determination of underemployment is significant. Both occupations and industrial sectors influence the likelihood of underemployment in America.

Neostructuralist authors (Beck et al., 1978; Averitt, 1988, 1968; O'Connor, 1979) within the dual economy tradition, conceptualize economic sectors as structural entities which derive from the nature of modern industrial capitalism. This framework differs from Piore (1975) and others in the dual labor market and labor force segmentation tradition who tend to define sectors, or segments, on the basis of the characteristics of labor markets and worker behavior. From the dual economy perspective, these labor market characteristics are seen as predictable outcomes of the sectoral structure, not as their defining characteristics.

Thus, the results of the estimation of the ordinal and the multinomial logit models suggest that the sectoral differences between core, state, and periphery have important implications for the opportunity structures and experiences faced by individual workers. The estimates of the ordinal model indicate that workers in the core and the state sectors of the economy tend to be less underemployed than the workers in the periphery.

The multinomial logit model offers even more detailed distinctions between economic sectors. Workers in both the state and the core sectors are less likely to be involuntary part-time or full-time low wage employed than in high wage full-time jobs, relative to periphery workers. But only state workers are less likely to be unemployed than having good jobs (full-time high wage) vis-a-vis periphery workers, since the likelihood of unemployment is the same for workers in the core and in the periphery. And finally, workers in the core are as likely to be discouraged as those workers in the periphery.

These results are interpreted from a neostructuralist perspective as meaning that in the core and state sectors, workers move within job structures characterized by differentiated task and wage schedules with often well defined career patterns, i.e., internal labor markets (Gordon, 1972; O'Connor, 1979; Beck et al., 1978; Doeringer and Piore, 1971). Formal education is widely used to mediate individual access to job ladders, and workers' outcomes, wages, underemployment, etc., are largely determined by their respective access to different job clusters, by the relatively rigid pattern of wages attached to the job structures through those structures (Gordon, 1972). In the peripheral sector, occupational opportunity structure is more restricted with a consequent dampening of task and wage variations. In this sector, variation in underemployment and wages will depend very little on variations in individual "capacities" like aptitude, reasoning and vocational skill (Gordon, 1972).

The significance of underemployment structural variation has important implications for the analysis of individual underemployment. Specifically, it implies that those analyses of underemployment which estimate the underemployment likelihood of individual characteristics such as schooling, social background, and work experience, without including controls for structural variables such as economic sectors, will produce results which are systematically biased through misspecification of the economic structure.

In providing a nonindividualistic alternative for the analysis of underemployment, neostructuralist theories provide structural explanations for economic differences between racial and sexual groups. Rather than interpreting group differences in underemployment as due to different rates of individual "failure" in a competitive market, the theory suggests that such group differences may be the outcome of differential assignments of group members within the sectoral structure of the economic order (Gordon, 1972; Bluestone, 1970).

If after controlling for human capital, industrial sectors, and occupations, ethnic and gender groups are still disadvantaged in terms of underemployment, as the coefficients for blacks (in both CPS 1990 and 1988 analyses), Mexicans (CPS, 1988) and women (CPS, 1990) indicate, the reason might be, as Doeringer and Piore (1971) suggest, discrimination within the firm or corporation, as commented above, in the assignment of different types of jobs to minorities (including women) and white male workers. For example, more involuntary part-time or full-time low wage jobs could be assigned to minorities than to white males; minorities could be assigned to different internal labor markets than white male workers in the core or state sectors; or else, more minority workers may suffer lay-offs or firings vis-a-vis white male workers.

Discrimination could also exist at the entry ports of firms due to ethnic or gender antagonism, as mentioned above, even in some firms of the periphery. A situation that may be accentuated during recessionary periods. This may cause the presence of significant female and black effects on underemployment after controlling for occupations and economic sectors.

The results for occupations support neostructuralists' expectations: blue collar and service workers are the most likely to suffer underemployment, particularly in those non-unionized settings. These workers have less political resources or organizational power. They are also more subject to direct control by supervisors, and are the easiest to substitute, which allows them less negotiation power.

For the opposite reasons, managers, professionals, executives, administrators, and technicians are less likely than blue collar workers, including crafts, to become underemployed.

In sum, workers in some sectors and occupations are more underemployed than others. Different processes and power resources may account for such differences, according to neostructuralism. However, such explanation for the presence of structural effects may not be the only one. One alternative is given by efficiency wage theories (Yellen, 1984; Katz, 1986; Thaler, 1989), which claim to be a generalization of some neostructuralist theories, such as economic dualism (Akerlof, 1984).

The significant presence of occupations and industrial sectors as determinants of underemployment can also be interpreted as supporting my extension of efficiency wage theories to underemployment, as Table 6.1 shows.

The results obtained indicate that, according to efficiency wage theories, there seem to exist two sectors in the economy. One with efficiency wages and jobs; and a second without them. The first sector is formed by the following industries: public administration, finance, insurance, real estate, medical, hospitals, and manufacturing. The second economic sector, without efficiency wages and jobs, is integrated into agriculture, fisheries, forestry, mining, construction, wholesales, retail trade, transportation, utilities, welfare, religious, education, and services (see Tables 5.2 and 5.3). Workers in the second sector tend to be more underemployed than workers in the first sector.

Using the multinomial logit model, a more detailed comparison of underemployment likelihood was performed between the state administration sector, taken as the baseline category, and the other industries (Chapter 4).

Such a comparison indicates that workers in agriculture, forestry, fisheries, construction, whole sales and retail trades are more likely to be unemployed, involuntary part-time or full-time low wage employed, but equally likely to be discouraged, with respect to state administration workers. Mining workers, on the other hand, are more likely to be unemployed than state workers, but equally likely to be in other underemployment categories. And transportation, communications, and public utilities workers are more likely to be involuntary part-time employed than state workers (Table 4.3).

According to these results, the industries within the efficiency wage and job sector need to offer higher wages and better jobs because they face some of the following problems:

Shirking; due to imperfect observability of worker performance and high costs of monitoring. Turnover; due to hiring and training costs. Adverse selection; due to imperfect observability of worker quality. Union threat; due to costs of replacing existing workforce that gives employees bargaining power. And gift exchange social norms; because morale and worker feelings of loyalty to the firm depend on perceived fairness of wages and having a full-time or a part-time job.

Critics of efficiency wage theories (Katz, 1986; England, 1992) argue that other strategies could eliminate some of the problems that high wages intend to erase. Firms could impose bonds to incoming workers, organize internal labor markets, or pay below worker marginal product initially; then later in their careers, have it returned in the form of wages above the value of their marginal product and/or in the form of a pension upon retirement. These measures could solve the effort elicitation problem.

Although imposing bonds is rarely used by firms (Katz, 1986), its implementation may be jeopardized by credit access problems among workers. The recourse of low initial wages, as Weiss (1990) contends, may affect the quality of workers the firm is able to hire, or it may be counterproductive to improve worker's physical fitness, as in the case of the nutrition efficiency wage model. However, Akerlofs (1984, 1982) sociological theory, based on norms of gift exchange between workers and employers, claims to be compatible with other theories that support alternative solutions to the worker cooperation problem, such as economic dualism (Averitt, 1988, 1968; O'Connor, 1979; Beck et al., 1978) and the dual labor market theory (Doeringer and Piore, 1971).

Thus, the explanations of underemployment differences across gender and ethnic groups obtained in the estimation of the models and based on differences in shirking, turnover, adverse selection, or union threat between these groups, face the theoretical problems noticed above, as well as several empirical problems. Differences in turnover, shirking, and unionization propensity between men and women, or between ethnic groups net of individual and structural factors, have been questioned extensively in the literature (England, 1992; Katz, 1986). The only version of efficiency wage theories that remains robust to such critics is the sociological normative theory of Akerlofs (1984, 1982). This theory implies that underemployment differences between these groups are due to sexist and racist norms followed by employers and employees. The effects of some of these racist or sexist norms will not disappear when controls for industrial sectors are included. This may be the case if different gender or ethnic groups are assigned separate internal labor markets or career ladders (Doeringer and Piore, 1971).

Interestingly, until now most structuralist arguments to explain worker outcomes have been based on economic arguments. Now, a theory developed by economists finds its basis on sociological ground, an indication of how the two fields are interrelated, and how relevant Sociology may become as an alternative theoretical source to explain economic problems (England, 1992; England and Farkas, 1988; Granovetter, 1981).

But despite the relative merits of structuralist theories, human capital theory is still challenging them. There are two important cases where structural variables are not significant in explaining underemployment, as it is shown in Table 6.1. The first is the case of Mexican workers in 1989 (Chapter 3); and the second is the case of discouraged workers (Chapter 4).

The results obtained using CPS (1990) data in both models, the ordinal logistic regression and the multinomial logit model, show that Mexicans have the same likelihood as non-Mexicans, mostly whites, of being underemployed. Furthermore, the only significant variables determining Mexican underemployment are human capital ones. Therefore, Mexican underemployment is due to low educational attainment and job experience of Mexican workers.

In a sample of N=25,916 workers between 16 and 64 years old from the Current Population Survey 1990, I found that Mexicans have lower educational and age means than blacks and whites in the US. This supports my findings that Mexicans tend to be less educated and younger, relative to the other ethnic groups compared in this study, and also shown by other researchers (Borjas and Tienda, 1985; De Freitas, 1991; Reimers, 1992).

Mexicans also have a higher high school dropout rate than all other groups in the population (Fligstein and Fernandez, 1985; De Freitas, 1991). This accentuates the deficit in human capital that Mexican workers take to the market. In addition to these disadvantages, many Mexicans are not born in the U.S.. Therefore, their lack of language skills is argued to be an obstacle in getting education or job experience (De Freitas, 1991; De Anda, 1991).

In a sample of Mexican immigrants interviewed in 1976, nearly 47 percent were between 16 and 24 years old. The mean age (27.6) was far below the U.S. average that year (39). Over 43 percent of the Mexicans interviewed had completed fewer than five years of schooling, and another 42 percent had only between five and eight years. Fewer than 1 percent had received any higher, postsecondary education, compared with over 27 percent of the American labor force in 1973. The lower the schooling level, the weaker the knowledge of English. Three out of four said they spoke it "very badly" or "not at all" and another 15.3 percent "not very well" (De Freitas, 1991; pp. 22-23).

In sum, the results for underemployment of Mexican workers, based on CPS (1990) data, indicate the absence of discrimination against them. What disqualifies these workers in the labor market appears to be their lack of education and experience. Given that overall Mexican workers are not capable of competing with highly qualified white workers, the former are not a threat for the latter, therefore, discrimination does not seem to be necessary to limit their access to good jobs.

However, the analysis of CPS (1988) data shows that Mexicans are more likely than whites to be underemployed, despite the inclusion of controls for human capital and structural variables. This second analysis shows that experience does not decrease the underemployment likelihood for Mexicans; only education seems to make a difference. Education decreases the likelihood of being in involuntary part-time or low wage full-time jobs, but it does not affect worker's likelihood of being discouraged or unemployed (Table 5.5).

The analysis of CPS (1988) data shows the importance of occupation and industry for Mexican workers. Those workers in managerial, professional, or technical occupations are less likely to be underemployed than those workers in other types of occupations, such as services, crafts, and farming. In addition, those Mexican workers in construction and sales industries tend to be more underemployed than workers in other type of industries. Furthermore, the same analysis shows that foreign Mexican workers are less likely to be discouraged or unemployed, but equally likely to be in involuntary part-time or low wage jobs than their Mexican American counterparts, possibly because American born Mexicans have a higher reservation wage than foreign Mexican workers. Nevertheless, if foreign origin approximates English language ability adequately, my results using CPS (1988) data may indicate that what really hurts Mexican workers in the labor market—more than their language disadvantage—is a combination of low human capital achievement, their average youth (relative to other ethnic groups), holding low status occupations, and their disproportionate presence in industries which do not shelter them from underemployment, such as agriculture, construction, services, and sales.

Thus, the possible presence of discrimination against Mexicans in the analysis based on CPS (1988), in contrast to the apparent absence of it in the previous results based on CPS (1990), may be related to the performance of the economy during the business cycle, which may prompt ethnic conflict against Mexicans following the processes commented above, during the recessionary phases of the economy.

Discouraged workers share the same problems that Mexican workers have: the lack of human capital qualifications. However, women have a higher share amongst the discouraged workers, according to the results obtained by the multinomial logit model. Buss and Redburn (1988) hypothesize, based on percentage tables, that discouraged workers tend to be older or younger, with low educational attainment, and have more women and minorities among their ranks than the unemployed, who tend to be white males with an educational level around the general average for the population.

Buss and Redburn (1988) do not test these hypotheses. However, my results indicate that effectively, human capital investments and gender are important determinants of discouragement. Women are more likely than men to be discouraged workers. But my results fail to confirm that blacks or Mexicans are more discouraged than whites. Thus, workers with poor qualifications may become discouraged when they are repeatedly rejected while searching for jobs. In the case of women, market discrimination may be an important factor of why more female than male workers give up looking for jobs.

In sum, structuralists' theories of underemployment are highly supported by my findings in both models. However, the primordial importance of human capital determinants for discouragement, and the variation in the significance of structural determinants for Mexican underemployment across the economic cycle, may indicate that labor market mechanisms are acting over the labor force distinctively across gender and ethnic groups. In the next section, I summarize my findings related to deindustrialization theory.

DEINDUSTRIALIZATION AND UNDEREMPLOYMENT

The results related to deindustrialization theory vary depending on which model is utilized. This shows the relevance of the discussion about the adequacy of each modeling alternative. As Table 6.1 summarizes, according to the ordinal logistic regression model, there is no difference in underemployment among the different geographic regions of the country. Thus, this model does not provide any supportive evidence in favor of deindustrialization theory.

The result obtained with the multinomial logit model show that relative to the Northeast, the reference category, workers in the Midwest are more likely to be involuntary part-time or full-time low wage employed rather than full-time high wage employed. However, the same workers are equally likely to be discouraged or unemployed rather than full-time high wage employed. Similarly, workers in the South relative to workers in the Northeast are more likely to be full-time low wage employed rather than full-time high wage workers, but equally likely to be in any of the other underemployment categories.

And finally, workers in the West compared with workers in the Northeast are equally likely to be in any of the underemployment categories rather than full-time high wage workers.

Thus, the multinomial logit model indicates that Midwest workers are more likely to be in two underemployment categories than Northeast workers, while workers in the South are only more likely to be in one underemployment category. Therefore, underemployment is present in the Midwest more than in the rest of the country, but it is also present in the South. In this sense, the multinomial logit model gives only partial support to industrialization theory.

Do my results constitute a serious blow to deindustrialization theory? Not at all. Deindustrialization theory could be modified keeping the central idea at its core. Burawoy (1979) hypothesizes that the advantage of workers in the core sector of the economy has declined. The reason is the new forms of control that capitalists exercise over their workers, that Burawoy calls "hegemonic despotic". This hypothesis, verified by Weakliem (1990), suggests that putting the processes of deindustrialization and decline of the core together, American workers are going to face higher probabilities of different forms of underemployment.

The type of underemployment that workers face varies across geographic regions. As my results show, workers in the South have higher probabilities of being full-time low wage employed than of having full-time high wage jobs, since traditionally despotic forms of control have been exercised there (Reich, 1981), and industries have flown to the South after leaving other regions, probably the Midwest and Northeast (Bluestone and Harrison, 1982). Also, the threat of leaving the country allows firms to have more power of negotiation against unions across the country (Bluestone and Harrison, 1982, 1988; Weakliem, 1990). In such a situation, it is not surprising that, going through an economic recession, underemployment spreads across the country. However, as my results show, the kind of underemployment faced by every geographic region varies.

Underemployment and discouragement are pervasive across all regions; but low wages in full-time jobs are more present in the Midwest and in the South. And the Midwest, going through a deindustrialization process suffers more involuntary part-time employment, probably because workers cannot get old type manufacturing jobs anymore, as they used to.

Thus, deindustrialization theory is not a rigid body of ideas. On the contrary, it is possible to integrate deindustrialization theory with other theorizations of the American economy. It certainly suggests a mechanism that goes along with World System theories (Chase-Dunn, 1983), since it offers a view of what happens within a developed national economy that confronts world wide competition. American Capitalism has to restructure itself by moving part of its industrial plant to foreign countries. Thus, the American standard of living may be one of the victims of global competition.

SUMMARY AND PERSPECTIVES

This study has shown that underemployment is not a unidimensional problem. It is not uniquely determined by individual characteristics. Therefore, it is unfair to blame the victims of underemployment. Rather, the way individuals become underemployed is a complex process that goes through both individual and structural dimensions.

The environment where workers are situated constrains their chances for good employment. Even if workers are individually well qualified, economic sector, geographic region, union, or occupation matter as determinants of labor market underemployment. But the study of underemployment also shows in how many ways the American labor force is stratified.

Labor segmentation may exist across gender and ethnic lines. Despite efforts to eliminate discrimination it may still be there, affecting minorities, including women. Nevertheless, this study also shows that the situation of minorities is not uniform, and if economic policy has to be implemented, it would have to be adapted to particular characteristics of distinct social groups, without neglecting the fact that some general social policy measures would benefit everybody, as in the case of general educational improvement.

Thus, the disadvantage in human capital characteristics that is so relevant for Mexicans indicates the acute problem that this minority group has to become educated, a conclusion that strongly supports bilingual education policies and programs.

Facing problems similar to the Mexicans are the discouraged workers, also lacking human capital that qualifies them to have access to jobs. My analysis shows that this is a problem of the very young, and here one may find a connection between delinquency and stratification, since these young discouraged workers may become very attracted toward illegal ways of making their living (Wilson, 1980, 1987).

Blacks and women, on the other hand, suffer underemployment due to lack of education, lack of job experience, and structural factors, further complicated by discrimination. At the very least, this study suggests that enforcement of anti-discriminatory legislation should be a priority.

Many of these measures of social policy depend on how successful the economy is going to be to sort the current recession. Will the American working class be able to struggle to stop capital flight and speculative investments? Is there a total backlash against the achievements won during the New Deal awaiting us?

For the time being, this study suggests future directions in research. One is the evolution of underemployment across the business cycle, since it is possible that the findings obtained in this study will vary depending upon the stage of the business cycle. For example, Schervish (1983) finds that there is an interaction between gender and unemployment type. Such interaction varies depending on the economic sector and changes across the business cycle. Similarly, I would expect that underemployment is affected differently by individual and structural determinants across the business cycle. Also, the differences in underemployment between workers in the periphery and workers in the core could be affected by the year considered, as in Schervish's (1983) study on unemployment.

A second question that my research suggests is the relative underemployment situation of different Latino groups: Cubans, Puerto Ricans, Mexicans, etc. The research on wages has shown that Latino groups are stratified. Cubans tend to have higher wages than Mexicans and Puerto Ricans; and Mexicans have a higher labor market participation than Puerto Ricans, but the former tend to receive lower wages than the latter (De Freitas, 1991; Reimers, 1992). Are Latino groups similarly stratified in terms of underemployment?

A third research vein is constituted by the need to study discouraged workers. Little work has been done on this group (Buss and Redburn, 1988). How are discouraged workers affected by the business cycle? What determines that an unemployed worker becomes discouraged? Is the deindustrialization process that affects some areas of the U.S. increasing the chances of unemployed workers to become discouraged? Answers to these questions have been suggested, but not tested, by Buss and Redburn (1988), as well as by this study, but further elaboration is necessary.

And finally, there is the problem of testing the mechanisms of the theories utilized in this study. Some hypotheses shown in Table 1.1 and several findings in Table 6.1 are compatible with different theories. Therefore, a test of the consequences of the theories has not been sufficient to distinguish among the distinct explanations for underemployment. It is necessary to go further and test the mechanisms advanced by the theories.

The test of theoretical mechanisms has originated discussion and controversy, particularly between neostructuralists and orthodox economists (Smith, 1990; Wright, 1979; Cain, 1976). But as long as the mechanisms that support the theories are not tested, neostructuralists' explanations are going to be as good as neoclassical ones.

Ways of solving this controversy have been suggested in the literature. Blackburn and Mann (1979) study a sample of British workers and conclude that internal labor markets are organized following bureaucratic hierarchical rules rather than neoclassical expectations of scarcity of qualified workers. To further contribute to the solution of the controversy between efficiency (neoclassical economic theory) and worker power (neostructuralism) as the motivation for building internal labor markets, research on the situation of labor under authoritarian regimes may be useful. For example, if during the Pinochet dictatorship in Chile (1973 - 1989) where worker power was taken to its minimal level, internal labor markets were still present, then alternative explanations for the need of internal labor markets may be necessary. Under these conditions, internal labor markets may have been dictated by efficiency considerations, as neoclassical economists have suggested (Smith, 1990), unless one proves that independently of how repressive a regime can be, it is impossible to rule worker power out of the factory.

This problem also suggests further questions: how is the stratification of the labor force affected by the type of regime? Is labor stratification influenced by the situation of the country in the world economy? and if it is, in what ways? Perhaps it is time for American stratification researchers to have a less ethnocentric focus and look at the semi-periphery and periphery of the world.

References

Abowd, John M., and Mark R. Killingsworth. 1985. "Employment, Wages, and Earnings of Hispanics in the Federal and Nonfederal Sectors: Methodological Issues and Their Empirical Consequences." Pp. 77-125 in *Hispanics in the U.S. Economy*, edited by G. J. Borjas and M. Tienda. California: Academic.

Aigner, Dennis J., and Glen G. Cain. 1977. "Statistical Theories of Discrimination in Labor Markets."*Industrial and Labor Relations Review* 30: 175-187.

Agresti, Alan. 1990. *Categorical Data Analysis*. New York: John Wiley and Sons.

Akerlof, George. 1984. "Gift Exchange and Efficiency Wage Theory: Four Views." *American Economic Review Proceedings*, May, 74: 79-83.

Akerlof, George. 1982. "Labor Contracts as Partial Gift Exchange." *Quarterly Journal of Economics*, November, 97: 54-569.

Averitt, Robert T.. 1968. *The Dual Economy*. New York, W.W. Norton.

Averitt, Robert T.. 1988. The Prospects for Economic Dualism. A Historical Perspective. In George Farkas and Paula England (eds.), *Industries, Firms and Jobs. Sociological and Economic Approaches*. New York: Plenum.

Azariadis, Costas. 1975. "Implicit Contracts and Underemployment Equilibria." *Journal of Political Economy* 83: 1183-1202.

Baron, James N.. 1984. "Organizational Perspectives on Stratification." In Ralph Turner (ed.), *Annual Review of Sociology*, Vol. 10. Palo Alto, CA: Annual Reviews.

Bean, Frank D., and M. Tienda. 1987. *The Hispanic Population of the United States*. New York: Russell Sage Foundation.

Baron, James N. and Andrew E. Newman. 1990. "For What It's Worth: Organizations, Occupations, and the Value of Work done by Women and Nonwhites." *American Sociological Review* 55: 155-75.

Beck, E.M., Patrick M. Horan, and Charles M. Tolbert II. 1980. "Stratification in a Dual Economy: A Sectoral Analysis of Earnings Determination." *American Sociological Review* 43: 794-20.

Becker, Gary S. 1964. *Human Capital: A Theoretical and Empirical Analysis*. New York, National Bureau of Economic Research.

Becker, Gary S. 1971. *The Economics of Discrimination*. Second Edition. Chicago: University of Chicago Press.

Becker, Gary S. 1975. *Human Capital: A Theoretical and Empirical Analysis, with Special Reference to Education*. Second Edition. Chicago: University of Chicago.

Beller, Andrea H., and John W. Graham. 1988. "The Feminization of Poverty. Child Support Payments: Evidence from Repeated Cross-Sections." *AEA Papers and Proceedings*: 81-85.

Berg, Ivar. 1970. *Education and Jobs: The Great Training Robbery*. New York: Praeger.

Bibb, Robert and William H. Form. 1977. "The Effects of Industrial, Occupational, and Sex-Stratification on Wages in Blue-Collar Markets." *Social Forces* 55: 974-96.

Blackburn, R. M., and Michael Mann. 1979. *The Working Class in the Labor Market*. London: MacMillan.

Blank, Rebecca M.. 1990. "Are Part-Time Jobs Bad Jobs?" In Gary Bartless (ed.), *A Future of Lousy Jobs?* Washington, D.C.: The Brookings Institution.

Blau, Francine and Lawrence Kahn. 1981. "Race and Sex Differences in Quits by Young Workers." *Industrial and Labor Relations Review*, vol. 34: 563-577.

Bluestone, Barry. 1970. "The Tripartite Economy: Labor Markets and the Working Poor." *Poverty and Human Resources* 5: 15-35.

Bluestone, Barry, and Bennett Harrison. 1980. *Corporate Flight: The Causes and Consequences of Economic Dislocation*. Washington, D.C., Institute for Policy Studies.

Bluestone, Barry, and Bennett Harrison. 1982. *The Deindustrialization of America*. New York: Basic Books.

Bluestone, Barry, and Bennett Harrison. 1988. "The Growth of Low-Wage Employment: 1963-86." *American Economic Review*, vol. 78: 124-128.

Bonacich, Edna. 1972. "A Theory of Ethnic Antagonism: The Split Labor Market," *American Sociological Review* 37, no. 5: pp.547-59.

Boyes, William J.. 1992. *Macroeconomics: Intermediate Theory and Policy*. Third Edition. Ohio: South-Western.

Bulow J. I. and Summers, L. H. 1986. "A Theory of Dual Labor Markets with Application to Industrial Policy, Discrimination and Keynesian Unemployment." *Journal of Labor Economics.*

Burawoy, Michael. 1979. *Manufacturing Consent.* Chicago: University of Chicago Press.

Burris, Val. 1983. "The Social and Political Consequences of Overeducation." *American Sociological Review* 48: 454-467.

Buss, Terry F. and F.S. Redburn. 1988. *Hidden Unemployment: Discouraged Workers and Public Policy.* New York: Praeger.

Cain, Glenn G.. 1976. "The Challenge of Segmented Labor Market Theories to Orthodox Theory: A Survey." *Journal of Economic Literature* 14: 1215-57.

Chamberlain, Neil W.. 1969. "Some Further Thoughts on the Concept of Human Capital", in *Cost-Benefit Analysis of Manpower Policies.* Edited by G.C. Somers and W.D. Wood. Madison: Industrial Relations Research Institute, University of Wisconsin, pp. 230-48.

Chase-Dunn, Christopher. 1983. "The Kernel of the Capitalist World-Economy: Three Approaches." Pp. 35-78 in *Contending Approaches in World-System Analysis*, edited by W. Thompson. Beverly Hills, CA: Sage.

Clogg, Clifford C.. 1979. *Measuring Underemployment: Demographic Indicators for the U.S..* New York, Academic.

Clogg, Clifford C., and Sullivan, Teresa. 1983. Labor Force Composition and Underemployment Trends, 1969-1980. Social Indicators Research: 117-152.

Clogg, Clifford C., Sullivan, T.A., and Mutchler, J.E.. 1986. "Measuring Underemployment and Inequality in the Work Force." *Social Indicators Research* 18: 375-93.

Cornfield, Daniel B.. 1981. "Industrial Social Organization and Layoffs in American Manufacturing Industry." In Ivar Berg (ed.), *Sociological Perspectives in Labor Markets.* New York: Academic Press, pp. 219-248.

Cornfield, Daniel. 1983. "Chances of Layoff in a Corporation: A Case Study." *Administration Science Quarterly*, vol. 28, pp. 503-520.

Davis, Kingley and Wilbert E. Moore. 1945. "Some Principles of Stratification." *American Sociological Review* 10: 242-249.

De Anda, Roberto Moreno. 1991. *Inequality at Work: A Comparison of Underemployment and Stratification Between Mexican-Origin and White Workers*. Unpublished Ph.D. Dissertation. Tucson, AZ: The University of Arizona.

DeFreitas, Gregory. 1991. *Inequality at Work:Hispanics in the U.S. Labor Force*. New York: Oxford University Press.

Dickens, William T. and K. Lang. 1985. "A Test of Dual Labor Market Theory." *American Economic Review* 75: 792-805.

Dickens, William T. and Lawrence F. Katz. 1987. "Inter-Industry Wage Differences and Industry Characteristics." In Kevin Lang and Jonathan S. Leonard (eds.), *Unemployment and the Structure of Labor Markets*. New York: Basil Blackwell.

Doeringer, Peter B., and Michael J. Piore. 1971. *Internal Labor Markets and Manpower Analysis*. Lexington, MASS.: Heath.

Duncan, Greg and Saul Hoffman. 1978. "On the Job Training and Earnings Differences by Race and Sex." *Review of Economics and Statistics*, vol. 61: 601.

Dunlop, John T.. 1957 "The Task of Contemporary Wage Theory," in *New Concepts in Wage Discrimination*. Edited by George W. Taylor and Frank C. Pierson. New York: McGraw-Hill, pp. 117-39.

Edwards, Richard C.. 1979, *Contested Terrain*. New York: Basic.

Ehrenberg, Ronald G., and Ronald L. Oaxaca. 1976. "Unemployment Insurance, Duration of Unemployment and Subsequent Wage Gain." *American Economic Review* 66: 754-66.

Ehrenberg, Ronald G., and Robert S. Smith. 1991. *Modern Labor Economics. Theory and Public Policy*. Fourth Edition. New York: Harper Collins.

Ehrenberg, Ronald G., and Robert S. Smith. 1988. *Modern Labor Economics: Theory and Public Policy*. ILL: Scott, Foresman, and Co.

England, Paula (ed.). 1993. *Theories of Feminism*. New York: Aldine de Gruyter.

England, Paula. 1992. *Comparable Worth: Theories and Evidence*. New York: Aldine de Gruyter.

England, Paula, and George Farkas. 1988. "Economic and Sociological Views of Industries, Firms, and Jobs", in George Farkas and Paula England (eds.), *Industries, Firms, and Jobs. Sociological and Economic Approaches*. New York: Plenum.

England, Paula, and George Farkas. 1986. *Households, Employment, and Gender: A Social, Economic and Demographic View*. New York: Aldine de Gruyter.

Farkas, George, and Paula England. 1985. "Integrating the Sociology and Economics of Employment, Compensation and Unemployment." In Richard Simpson and Ida Simpson (eds.), *Research in the Sociology of Work, Vol. 3: Unemployment.* Greenwich, CT.: JAI Press.

Farkas, George, and Paula England (eds.). 1988. *Industries, Firms and Jobs. Sociological and Economic Approaches.* New York: Plenum.

Farkas, George, Paula England, and Margaret Barton. 1988. "Structural Effects on Wages. Sociological and Economic Views". In George Farkas, and Paula England (eds.), *Industries, Firms, and Jobs. Sociological and Economic Approaches.* New York: Plenum.

Featherman, David and Robert Hauser. 1978. *Opportunity and Change.* New York: Academic.

Feldstein, Martin S.. 1973. "The Economics of the New Unemployment," *The Public Interest* 33: 3-42.

Feldstein, Martin S.. 1975. "The Importance of Temporary Layoffs: An Empirical Analysis," *Brookings Papers on Economic Activity 3.*

Feldstein, Martin S.. 1976. "Temporary Layoffs in the Theory of Unemployment," *Journal of Political Economy* 84: 937-58.

Fisher, Lloyd, 1953. *The Harvest Labor Market in California.* MASS: Harvard University Press.

Fligstein, Neil, Alexander Hicks, and S. Phillip Morgan. 1983. "Toward a Theory of Income Determination." *Work and Occupations* 10: 289-306.

Form, William H., and Joan A. Huber. 1976 "Occupational Power." Pp. 751-806 in *Handbook of Work, Organization, and Society,* edited by Robert Durkin. Chicago: Rand McNally.

Friedman, Milton. 1962. *Capitalism and Freedom.* Chicago: University of Chicago.

Galbraith, John K.. 1987. *Economics in Perspective: A Critical History.* Boston: Houghton Mifflin.

Gordon, David M.. 1972. *Theories of Poverty and Underemployment.* Lexington, MA: Heath.

Granovetter, Mark. 1981. "Toward a Sociological Theory of Income Differences." Pp. 11-47 in I. Berg (ed.), *Sociological Perspectives on Labor Markets.* New York: Academic Press.

Green, Christopher. 1990. *Canadian Industrial Organization and Policy.* Third Edition. Toronto: McGraw-Hill Ryerson.

Grenier, Gilles. 1984. "The Effects of Language Characteristics on the Wages of Hispanic-American Males." Journal of Human Resources 19: 53-71.

Hall, Robert E.. 1970. "Recent Increases in Unemployment." *Brookings Papers on Economic Activity* 1: 147-150.

Hall, Richard H.. 1986 *Dimensions of Work*. Beverly Hills, CA: Sage.

Hamermesh, Daniel S., and Albert Rees. 1988. *The Economics of Work and Pay*. New York: Harper and Row.

Hanushek, Eric A., and John E. Jackson. 1977. *Statistical Methods for Social Scientists*. New York: Academic.

Hauser, Philip M.. 1972. "The Work Force in Developing Areas," Ivar Berg (ed.), *Human Resources and Economic Welfare: Essays in Honor of Eli Ginsberg*, New York and London: Columbia University Press, pp. 142-162.

Hauser, Philip M.. 1974. "The Measurement of Labor Utilization." *Malayan Economic Review* 19: 1-17.

Hauser, Philip M.. 1977. "The Measurement of Labor Utilization-More Empirical Results." *Malayan Economic Review* 22: 10-25.

Hauser, Robert M., and David Featherman. 1977. *The Process of Stratification*. New York: Academic Press.

Hausman, Jerry and Daniel McFadden. 1984."Specification Tests for the Multinomial Logit Model". *Econometrica*, Vol. 52, No. 5: 1219-1240.

Hausman, J.A. and D.A. Wise. 1978. "A Conditional Probit Model for Qualitative Choice: Discrete Decisions Recognizing Interdependence and Heterogeneous Preferences", *Econometrica*, 46: 403-426.

Hill, M.S.. 1983. "Trends in the Economic Situation of U.S. Families and Children: 1970-1980." In R.R. Nelson and F. Skidmore (eds.), *American Families and the Economy*, pp. 9-58. Washington, D.C.: National Academy Press.

Hodson, Randy. 1984. "Companies, Industries, and the Measurement of Economic Segmentation." *American Sociological Review* 49: 335-348.

Hodson, Randy. 1983. *Workers Earnings and Corporate Economic Structure*. New York: Academic.

Hodson, Randy D.. 1977. *Labor Force Participation and Earnings in the Core, Peripheral, and State Sectors of Production*, M. A. thesis, Department of Sociology, University of Wisconsin, Madison.

Hodson, Randy and Paula England. 1986. "Industrial Structure and Sex Differences in Earnings." *Industrial Relations*, Vol. 25, No. 1: 16-32.

Hodson, Randy and Robert L. Kaufman. 1982. "Economic Dualism: A Critical Review." *American Sociological Review* 47: 727-739.

Hutchison, D.. 1984. "Ordinal Variable Regression Using the McCullagh (Proportional Odds) Model." *GLIM Newsletter* 9: 9-17.

Kalleberg, Arne L.. 1988. "Comparative Perspectives on Work Structures and Inequality." *Annual Review of Sociology* 14: 203-25.

Kalleberg, Arne L.. 1989. "Linking Macro and Micro Levels: Bringing Workers Back into the Sociology of Work." *Social Forces* 67: 582-92.

Kalleberg, Arne L. and Ivan Berg. 1987.*Work and Industry: Structures, Markets, and Processes*. New York: Plenum.

Kalleberg, Arne L. and Aage B. Sorensen. 1979. "The Sociology of Labor Markets." *Annual Review of Sociology* 5: 351-79.

Kalleberg, Arne L., Michael Wallace and Robert P. Althauser. 1981. "Economic Segmentation, Worker Power, and Income Inequality." *American Journal of Sociology* 87: 651-83.

Kalleberg, Arne and Ivar Berg. 1987. *Work and Industry: Structures, Markets, and Processes*. New York: Plenum.

Kasarda, John D.. 1983. "Entry-Level Jobs, Mobility, and Urban Minority Unemployment." *Urban Affairs Quarterly* 19: 21-40.

Katz, Lawrence F.. 1986. "Efficiency Wage Theories: A Partial Evaluation." *National Bureau of Economic Research Working Paper Series* No. 1906.

Kaufman, Robert L.. 1981. *Racial Discrimination and Labor Market Segmentation*. Unpublished Ph.D. dissertation, Department of Sociology, University of Wisconsin at Madison.

Kaufman, Robert L., Randy Hodson and Neil D. Fligstein. 1981. "Defrocking Dualism: a New Approach to Defining Industrial Sectors." *Social Science Research* 10: 1-31.

Keynes, John Maynard. 1936. *The General Theory of Employment Interest and Money*. New York: Harcourt, Brace.

Kiefer, Nicholas, and George Neumann. 1979. "An Empirical Job Search Model with a Test of the Constant Reservation Wage Hypothesis," *Journal of Political Economy* 87: 89-107.

Killinsgworth, Charles C.. 1963. "Automation, Jobs, and Manpower: Statement," in *Nation's Manpower Revolution*. Senate Hearing. Subcommittee on Employment and Manpower of the Committee on Labor and Public Welfare, 88th Congress, 1st Session. Washington: U.S.G.P.O., pp. 1476-94.

Killingsworth, Charles C.. 1974 "Unemployment: A Fresh Perspective." Pp. 97-102 in L.G. Reynolds, S.H. Masters, and C. Moser (eds.), *Readings in Labor Economics and Labor Relations*. Englewood Cliffs: Prentice Hall. A Prepared Statement Before the Joint Committee, August 6, 1971, U.S. Congress.

Killingsworth, Charles C. and Christopher T. King. 1977. "Tax Cuts and Employment Policy." Pp. 1-33 in R. Taggart (ed.), *Job Creation: What Works?* Salt Lake City: Olympus.

Kirschenman, Joleen, and Kathryn M. Neckerman. 1991. "'We'd Love to Hire Them, But...': The Meaning of Race for Employers." In Christopher Jencks and Paul E. Peterson (eds.), *The Urban Underclass*. Washington, D.C.: The Brookings Institution.

Klein, Bruce W. and Philip L. Rones. 1989. "A Profile of The Working Poor." *Monthly Labor Review* (October): 3-13.

Kniesner, Thomas J., Marjorie B. McElroy, and Steven Wilcox. 1988. "Getting into Poverty Without a Husband, and Getting Out, With or Without."*American Economic Review, Papers and Proceedings*, vol. 78: 86-95.

Krueger, Alan B. and Lawrence H. Summers. 1988. "Efficiency Wages and The Inter-Industry Wage Structure." *Econometrica*, vol.56: 259-293.

Krueger, Alan B. and Lawrence H. Summers. 1987. "Reflections on the Inter-Industry Wage Structure." In Kevin Lang and Jonathan S. Leonard (eds.), *Unemployment and the Structure of Labor Markets*. New York: Basil Blackwell.

Levitan, Ṣar, Garth Magnum, and Ray Marshall. 1981. *Human Resources and Labor Markets*. New York: Harper and Row, Inc.

Lang, Kevin and William T. Dickens. 1988. "Neoclassical and Sociological Perspectives on Segmented Labor Markets." In Farkas, George and Paula England (eds.), *Industries, Firms and Jobs. Sociological and Economic Approaches*. Plenum Press: New York.

Lichter, Daniel T.. 1988. "Racial Differences in Underemployment in American Cities." *American Journal of Sociology* 93 (4): 771-92.

Malcolmson, J.. 1984. "Work Incentives, Hierarchy, and Internal Labor Markets." *Journal of Political Economy* 92: 486-507.

Marx, Karl and Friedrich Engels. 1964. *The Communist Manifesto.* New York: Modern Reader Paperbacks.

Marx, Karl. 1967. Capital: *A Critique of Political Economy. Vol. I.* New York: International Publishers.

Maddala, G.S.. 1983. *Limited-Dependent and Qualitative Variables in Econometrics.* Cambridge: Cambridge University Press.

McFadden, Daniel. 1974. "Conditional Logit Analysis of Qualitative Choice Behaviour", in P. Zambreka, ed., *Frontiers in Econometrics,* Academic, New York: 105-142.

Mincer, Jacob. 1962. "On-the-Job Training: Costs, Returns, and Some Implications." *Journal of Political Economy* 70 (5; Part 2: Supplement): 50-79.

Mitchell, Wesley C.. 1927. *Business Cycles.* New York: National Bureau of Economic Research.

Murphy, K. M. and R. Topel. 1986. "Unemployment, Risk, and Earnings: Testing for Equalizing Wage Differences in the Labor Market." Mimeo, UCLA (March).

Myrdal, Gunnar. 1968. *Asian Drama.* New York, Pantheon.

Nardone, Thomas J.. 1986. "Part-time Workers: Who Are They?" *Monthly Labor Review,* vol. 109 (February): 13-19.

Numerical Algorithms Group. 1979. *GLIM Newsletters* Oxford: Oxford University Press.

O'Connor, James. 1973. *The Fiscal Crisis of The State.* New York: St. Martin's Press.

Oi, Walter. 1962. "Labor as a Quasi-Fixed Factor." *Journal of Political Economy* 70: 538-555.

Okun, Arthur M.. 1962. "Potential GNP: Its Measurement and Significance." *Proceedings of the Business and Economic Statistics Section, American Statistical Association*: 98-104.

Parsons, Donald O.. 1972. "Specific Human Capital: An Application to Quit Rates and Layoff Rates." *Journal of Political Economy* 80: 1120-1143.

Piore, Michael. 1975. "Notes for a Theory of Labor Market Stratification." Pp. 125-50 in Richard C. Edwards, Michael Reich and David M. Gordon (eds.), *Labor Market Segmentation.* Lexington, MA: Heath.

Portes, Alejandro. 1989. "Latin American Urbanization during the Years of the Crisis". *Latin American Research Review* XXIV, No.3. Albuquerque: New Mexico.

Poterba, J. and L. H. Summers. 1984. "Adjusting the Gross Changes Data: Implications for Labor Market Dynamics." *National Bureau of Economic Research Working Paper* No. 1436 (August).

Przeworski, Adam. 1977. "The Process of Class Formation from Karl Kautsky's 'The Class Struggle' to Recent Debates." *Politics and Society* 7: 343-403.

Rees, Albert. 1973. *The Economics of Work and Pay*. New York: Harper and Row.

Reich, Michael, 1981. *Racial Inequality: A Political-Economic Analysis*. New Jersey: Princeton.

Reich, Michael. 1971. "The Economics of Racism." Pp. 107-113 in David M. Gordon (ed.), *Problems in Political Economy*. Lexington, MA: Heath.

Reich, Michael, David M. Gordon and Richard C. Edwards. 1973. "A Theory of Labor Market Segmentation." *American Economic Review* 63: 359-65.

Rumberger, Robert. 1980. "The Impact of Surplus Schooling on Productivity and Earnings." *The Journal of Human Resources* 22: 24-50.

SAS Institute Inc.. 1986. *SUGI Supplemental Library User's Guide, Version 5 ed.* Cary, NC: SAS Institute, Inc.

Schervish, Paul G.. 1983. *The Structural Determinants of Unemployment: Vulnerability and Power in Market Relations*. New York: Academic Press.

Shank, Susan E.. 1986. "Preferred Hours of Work and Corresponding Earnings." *Monthly Labor Review*, vol. 109 (November): 40-44.

Shannon, Thomas R.. 1989. *An Introduction to the World-System Perspective*. Westview Press

Smith, Michael R.. 1990. "What is New in 'New Structuralists' Analyses of Earnings?" *American Sociological Review*, vol. 55: 827-841.

Solon, Gary. 1985. "Work Incentive Effects of Taxing Unemployment Benefits. " *Econometrica* 53: 295-306.

Sorensen, Aage B.. 1983. "Sociological Research on the Labor Market: Conceptual and Methodological Issues." *Work and Occupations* 10: 261-87.

Sorensen, Aage B. and Arne L. Kalleberg. 1981. "An Outline of a Theory of the Matching of Persons to Jobs." In Ivar Berg (ed.), *Sociological Perspectives in Labor Markets*. New York: Academic Press, pp. 49-74.

Spence, Michael A.. 1973. "Job Market Signaling." *Quarterly Journal of Economics* 87, 3: 355-374.

Stigler, George J.. 1961. "The Economics of Information." *Journal of Political Economy* 69: 213-225.

Stigler, George J.. 1962. "Information in the Labor Market. "*Journal of Political Economy* 50, 5 (Part 2: Supplement, October): 94-105.

Stinson, John F.. 1986."Moonlighting by Women Jumped to Record Highs." *Monthly Labor Review*, vol. 109 (November): 22-25.

Sullivan, Teresa, 1978. Marginal Workers: Marginal Jobs: *The Underutilization of American Workers*. Austin: The University of Texas Press.

Thaler, Richard H.. 1989. "Anomalies: Interindustry Wage Differentials." *Journal of Economic Perspectives*, vol. 3: 181-193.

The Economist. 1991. November 2nd-8th.

Thurow, Lester C.. 1975. *Generating Inequality*. New York: Basic Books.

Tiggs, Leann M.. 1987. *Changing Fortunes: Industrial Sectors and Workers' Earnings*. New York: Praeger.

Tiggs, Leann M.. 1988. "Age, Earnings, and Change Within the Dual Economy." *Social Forces* 66: 676-98.

Tilly, Chris. 1991. "Reasons for The Continuing Growth of Part-Time Employment." *Monthly Labor Review* (March): 10-32.

U.S. Bureau of the Census. 1990. *Statistical Abstract of the United States (110th edition)*. Washington, D.C.

U.S. Department of Commerce. 1990. *Current Population Survey: Annual Demographic File*. U.S. Department of Commerce, Bureau of the Census.

U.S. Department of Commerce. 1988. *Current Population Survey: Fertility, Birth Expectations, and Immigration File*. U.S. Department of Commerce, Bureau of the Census.

Weakliem, David L.. 1990. "Relative Wages and The Radical Theory of Relative Segmentation." *American Sociological Review*, Vol. 55: 574-590.

Weiss, Andrew. 1990. *Efficiency Wages: Models of Unemployment, Layoffs, and Wage Dispersion*. New Jersey: Princeton University Press.

Welch, Finis. 1973. "Black-White Differences in Returns to Schooling." *American Economic Review* 63: 893-907.

Williamson, Oliver E., Michael Wachter, and Jeffrey Harris. 1975. "Understanding the Employment Relationship:The Analysis of Idiosyncratic Exchange." *Bell Journal of Economics* 6: 250-278.

Wilson, William J.. 1980. *The Declining Significance of Race. Blacks and Changing American Institutions.* Chicago: University of Chicago Press.

Wilson, William J.. 1987. *The Truly Disadvantaged.* The Inner City, the Underclass, and Public Policy. Chicago: University of Chicago Press.

Wright, Erik Olin. 1978. *Class, Crisis and the State.* London: New Left Books.

Wright, Erik Olin. 1979. *Class Structure and Income Determination.* New York: Academic Press.

Wright, Erik Olin. 1980. "Class and Occupation." *Politics and Society* 9: 177-214.

Yellen, Janet L.. 1984. "Efficiency Wage Models of Unemployment." *American Economic Review Proceedings*, May, 74: 200-205.

Index

Printed in the United States
by Baker & Taylor Publisher Services